"AN EXCELLENT GUIDE TO
ENTREPRENEURING." —*Library Journal*

The historical formula for the entrepreneur has
been to start a business, build it up, sell out, get
out, and start the cycle again. But now there's a
new breed of entrepreneur who sticks with his or
her venture and keeps on innovating. With Steven
C. Brandt's rare combination of business
management and academic expertise behind it,
here is the only guide you'll ever need to this new
orate strategy, your own personal
for developing *and* managing a
any.

epreneuring

ell organized and easy to follow
the major and minor factors
essential to making a business successful."
—*Concise Books Reviews*

STEPHEN C. BRANDT is currently Senior
Lecturer in Management at the Stanford School
of Business. Dr. Brandt is an experienced CEO
and corporate director, and is the author of
*Entrepreneuring: in Established Companies:
Managing Toward the Year 2000,* which is
available in Signet paperback.

Entrepreneuring
The Ten Commandments for Building a Growth Company

STEPHEN C. BRANDT

A MENTOR BOOK

For my wife, Wooly,
and the vital new crop of entrepreneurs
breaking out around the world . . .

MENTOR
Published by the Penguin Group
Penguin Books USA Inc., 375 Hudson Street,
New York, New York 10014, U.S.A.
Penguin Books Ltd, 27 Wrights Lane,
London W8 5TZ, England
Penguin Books Australia Ltd, Ringwood,
Victoria, Australia
Penguin Books Canada Ltd, 2801 John Street,
Markham, Ontario, Canada L3R 1B4
Penguin Books (N.Z.) Ltd, 182-190 Wairau Road,
Auckland 10, New Zealand

Penguin Books Ltd, Registered Offices:
Harmondsworth, Middlesex, England

Published by arrangement with Addison-Wesley Publishing Company

First Mentor Printing, May, 1983
14 13 12 11 10 9 8 7

REGISTERED TRADEMARK—MARCA REGISTRADA

Library of Congress Catalog Card Number: 83-60249

Printed in the United States of America

Contents

Introduction

This book is written to be used. Entrepreneurship is undergoing a revival across the country. It's even being applauded overseas. Terms like innovation, technology, productivity, and startup are already part of everyday conversation. Seers write of a "third wave," a third giant step forward in the march of humankind, a step already in motion that will rival the agricultural and industrial revolutions which fueled much of our present-day material prosperity. Venture capitalists are suddenly national heroes as young microcomputer and biomed companies go public and make capital gains respectable, even patriotic, again. Engineers, middle managers, latent inventors, ambitious dropouts, blocked executives, tentative scientists, and MBAs frustrated with consulting and desk-jockey work find they can no longer suppress the itch to "go for it" as predictions and fears give way to the fact of turbulent times. They accurately sense that the timing for scratching the itch is as good as it is ever going to be.

Change favors entrepreneuring, and as the 1980s slip by like clouds, there's plenty of big change to go around. The challenge is to take advantage of it, and history will show that between now and 2000 A.D., most of the psychic and financial prizes will once again have gone to the bright and the bold who systematically generated fresh services, products, and experiences for discrete segments of our increasingly pluralistic society.

This book is not based on the premise that the 1960s (or the early 1900s, or the mid-1800s) are going to come again. This book *is* based on the premise that an increasingly well-educated, healthy, and enviro-energy-conscious population will stimulate and support a continuing flow of new industrial and consumer business opportunities that are compatible with the worldwide realities of the times. Those realities do not need to be spelled out here. Suffice it to say that successful entrepreneuring in the 1980s and 1990s must be in harmony with inflation, population dynamics, communications technology, major political and social trends, computers in the home, economic gyrations, floating exchange rates, and a world where each country aggressively rubs elbows with most others. For many people, these realities are problems. For entrepreneurs, they are "opportunities in disguise." Entrepreneuring is a cramped way of life in a static society.

In the pages that follow I have tried to present in a readable and usable fashion ten main *operating* principles or ideas for starting and managing a growth company. Several caveats are in order. First, the ten commandments are aimed at people involved with growth companies, i.e., companies with founders or managers intent on building a bigger enterprise, hopefully much bigger! I have little experience with the wonderful world of boutiques, consulting, or family restaurants. Such enterprises—typically based on very personalized service—add spice to the times and will probably flourish in the years ahead. Power to them. I can only say that I did not have them specifically in mind as I fashioned the ten commandments out of my own failures, successes, so-sos, and observations during the last sixteen years.

A second caveat is that the contents of this book are aimed at what I consider to be the mainline operating issues. No attempt is made to even touch upon the myriad of other important matters connected with launching a successful enterprise and staying out of court or jail due to indiscretions pertaining to withholding taxes, partners, stockholders, spouses, customers, or employees. There is a wealth of information available on what is generally called "small business management." Sources as diverse as the SBA (Small Business Administration), your local bank, trade associations, well-meaning institutes, countless college professors, and your local attorney annually pump out scores of pamphlets, books, and seminars on what I consider to be the administrative side of entrepreneuring. Make no mistake, administrative issues such as incorporation mechanics, filing for licenses, and obtaining workman's compensation insurance are vital. Treat them lightly only at your peril. This book, however, is not the source of guidance. Competent insurance people, attorneys, and accountants who have *verifiable experience* (check their references) with successful young companies are what you need.

The final caveat is that the ten commandments, even followed to the letter, will not automatically make you rich, beautiful, handsome, fulfilled, or whatever. I wish it could be otherwise, but the record indicates that the primary requirements for success are an identifiable and receptive market, a "better mousetrap," sufficient capital, a balanced team to lead the way, tenacity, and thoughtful timing (some people call it luck). The ten commandments do aim to help you weave these ingredients together in a pragmatic way and to avoid some of the more common operating mistakes entrepreneurs tend to make during those early years when their young companies lack momentum and are still vulnerable to sudden failure from stockholder squabbles, unclear objectives, a short-term negative cash flow, or an absence of functional talent.

Organized or institutionalized entrepreneurship is a relatively new phenomenon. Seminars and college courses on the subject have only begun to be offered in the last few years. Venture capital is just now gravitating to a position of legitimacy as a full-time, professional occupation of importance to the nation. Government for the first time is taking note that new business formation is not just an academic idea but, in fact, the major proven and sustaining source of new jobs. Capital gains is enjoying a resurgence of respectability again. And technology, which has traditionally been converted by entrepreneurs into things people buy, is increasingly thought to be the United States' number one economic weapon in a tough competitive world. These are heady times for both declared and still undecided entrepreneurs. The commandments that follow can help you think about the fundamentals for winning when you are your own boss.

Commandments one, two, and three cover key startup issues: Who should be involved? What are you out to accomplish? Who is going to buy what you are selling? Answers to these questions can save many a false start and point the way to creating a rock-like foundation for your new enterprise . . . if it's justified.

Commandment four includes, "Guide to Preparing a Business Plan." If you wish to build a business of any complexity at all, you should have a written plan; if you wish to attract outside money from people other than your friends and relatives, you must have a written plan; if you want to maximize your chances for building a viable, moneymaking enterprise without ruining your health in the process, you will have a written plan that has been critiqued by competent individuals whose opinions you respect.

Commandments five through eight deal with day-to-day operating matters that confront the senior people attempting to implement a (written) growth plan. Staffing, rewarding, extending the company, and paying the bills as you go are like blocking, passing, running, and tackling in football. The team that executes well will tend to win its share of games.

Finally, commandments nine and ten are aimed at salting entrepreneuring with a modicum of professionalism. The term professionalism denotes objectivity and detachment in the vocational matters at hand. Entrepreneurship has long and properly been associated with "sweat equity," an unyielding dedication that often leads to a merging of the identities of the founder(s) and the enterprise itself. Such a merging sometimes makes for certain efficiencies, but it is almost certain to limit a growth company over the longer run. The entrepreneur has but two choices when his or her enterprise successfully grows up—either change and grow with it or stop succeeding. Knowing when and how to change requires at least a half-an-arm's-length relationship with the budding business entity itself. The company is the company; you are you. They are not the same entity. Working from a proper business plan (commandment four) can help maintain this separation.

Just a few last words on philosophy. I have long thought that entrepreneuring was a life-style choice, and most of the high-rise company founders, officers, and venture capitalists who have contributed to the ideas in this book have tended to support that line of thinking. The 1960s formula was for the entrepreneur to start something, build it up, sell out, get out, and start the cycle again. But I think now that a new day is dawning. The 1980s breed of entrepreneur tends to be part of an entrepreneurial team that sticks with the ship and, more importantly, keeps on innovating. The result is a new corps of medium-sized companies such as Tandem Computer, First United Bancorporation, Triad Systems, Cdex, Intelligenetics, and Apple, that may well be prototypes of the successful corporations of the future. So the call to the entrepreneur is less "be your own boss" and somewhat more "let's build something fresh of value" than it used to be. Such circumstance does not in any way diminish the need and opportunity for the classic, one-person band, it only broadens the doorway in the legitimate entrepreneur's club.

It's a fine club. Entrepreneuring *is* a spirited way of life. The ten commandments are aimed at expanding the membership.

—STEVEN C. BRANDT
Palo Alto & Tahoe City,
California

1

The First Commandment

Limit the number of primary participants to people who can consciously agree upon and contribute directly to that which the enterprise is to accomplish, for whom, and by when.

There are many reasons people become involved in young, growing companies as owners, investors, or key employees. The broad range of satisfactions sought runs from an opportunity for personal expression on one end of the spectrum to capital gains on the other. Unless there is compatibility between what each primary participant wants out of the business, debilitating conflict is likely to ensue. The process of trying to consciously agree on the purpose of the enterprise is often difficult and revealing.

The primary participants of a new enterprise are those people who share in the initial ownership and/or management decision-making process of the company. The early days of a new company are critical days in which the tone and shape of the venture during its formative startup period are determined. If the tone or shape is convoluted by too much compromise or scarred by too much acrimonious debate, the foundation upon which the business is to be built will be less sturdy than it could and should be.

Here is a list of six common mistakes that would-be entrepreneurs often make in piecing together participants at the start of a new venture:

- The founding group is formed spontaneously
- The family or personal lawyer, insurance agent, CPA, and banker are automatically used as advisers
- Harmony is sought at the expense of creative conflict
- Needed administrative people are given stock in lieu of salary
- The board of directors consists solely or primarily of insiders—company officers, their spouses, and friends
- People with widely varying motives are mixed together in the same financial lifeboat

Let's consider these six common mistakes in a bit more depth.

The founding group is formed spontaneously. It doesn't take a novelist to portray a buzzing weekend cocktail party or an animated, after-work conversation at a bar during which a new product or service or distribution idea suddenly materializes and grows wings. It's a euphoric moment, and the two, three, or more souls standing in the circle are each caught up in the conception. Too often, they are also included willy-nilly as investors or key employees in the new venture that follows.

The spontaneous combination of souls may be just what the venture needs; then again, it may not be. The choice of investors and staff ideally should flow from a thorough understanding of the requirements for success in the prospective business. Essentially random collections of folks seldom make the right bedfellows for business building even if they are coworkers, classmates, or professional cousins.

How does an entrepreneur go about exploring an idea and triggering enthusiasm and interest, while at the same time reaching the ideal of limiting the number of primary participants to those who can consciously agree upon and contribute directly to that which the enterprise is to accomplish? *Gingerly* is perhaps the best adverb. The proper mindset is one that says that the eventual blueprint for building the business (the business plan) will dictate the desired specifications for investors and staff alike. If a small, qualified group can be organized to formulate the blueprint with a clear understanding from the start that everyone may not make the construction team if the bid is won, then the spontaneity risk is at least addressed.

Here is an illustration of how commandment one was violated because of an incompatibility of interests in the founding group.

> **CASE A.** A bright, energetic high school dropout conceived a new running shoe for the jogger market. He told and sold his uncle, an accountant, on the concept. Together they obtained close to $100,000 from individual outside investors, mostly friends who were avid joggers. The $100,000 represented essentially all the capital put into the company. The shoe was introduced to the market and sold very well. The company became a local success story. The outside investors wanted to plow back earnings and expand. The founder/president wanted to play with new shoe designs, do research and development, and give speeches on entrepreneurship at luncheon club meetings. The uncle/general manager was happy with $50,000 a year and a lot of stock on option. The company stagnated and eventually faltered. No one won. The founder lost his hero status; the uncle, his interesting job; the investors, their money. Each participant had his or her eye on a different star (. . . that which the enterprise is to accomplish, for whom . . .).

Common mistake number two has to do with guidance on administrative matters.

The family or personal lawyer, insurance agent, CPA, and banker are automatically used as advisers. Growth companies don't just happen. There is a lot of administrative expertise needed to glue the pieces together and keep the enterprise on a peaceful course among the snags and shoals of government requirements and legal practice. Any average attorney, CPA, or insurance agent can speak the language, give you advice, mail you something to sign, and send a bill. Not many have the professional interest and *proven experience* to help you build a company. It's a relatively narrow spectrum of practice. You have enough to do without investing in your advisers' educations.

In every major metropolitan area there are CPAs, attorneys, and insurance people who have developed or are developing a reputation with embryonic companies. Seek them out. Interview them. Discuss fees. Check their references. Then select who you want and listen to what they have to say. Your job as a modern entrepreneur is not to have all the answers, but to know where to get them. (How to insure that you ask the right questions is covered later in this chapter.)

Now what about bankers? In general, most of them do not have particular, in-depth expertise in business building, although in the 1980s they are learning quickly, out of necessity. Good bankers know about money, particularly debt money. And in commandment eight you will be advised to cultivate all your potential money sources on a continuing basis. So developing a working relationship with a reputable banker can be a useful activity. But don't confuse it with developing a financial plan for your new enterprise. For a financial plan you need assistance from someone skilled in corporate finance—particularly startup and small business financing. Some investment bankers, venture capitalists, and occasionally business school professors of finance or accounting may be helpful. Someone who has worked with the "numbers" and lived through a startup or two in the same field as your own is probably the best single source of guidance.

Harmony is sought at the expense of creative conflict. Entrepreneurs by nature tend to listen most attentively to themselves. In today's competitive world, as a gesture toward openmindedness, they may well seek the counsel of others. But there is a human tendency to seek out only what you want to hear. ("Yes, Steve, you're right. That is a *huge*, untapped market.") Experience indicates, however, that bad news costs a lot less if you get it sooner rather than later.

The primary participants in a new enterprise should bring a balanced, thoughtful view to the decision-making process. This precludes yespeople as well as those unqualified to make a direct contribution to the matters at hand.

> CASE B. A group of three prominent, academic scientists spotted a major opportunity in the emerging biomed industry. Technically it was within their combined spheres of influence. They mulled over the opportunity for nearly a year and then happened onto a young MBA student (with no biomed experience) in search of a field project for one of his classes. The student developed for them an elaborate business plan with computer-generated projections covering every conceivable angle. The four people got along well together in both business and social settings. The projections looked good. Four months later financing was obtained from an overseas

venture capital firm and the MBA was hired on as the general manager of the new company. Ask yourself: How reliable were the projections? (Recall, they were developed for the scientists, not by them.) How well qualified is the new general manager to build a competitive biomed company around the scientists' skills? How could some creative conflict among the participants have been beneficially woven into the formative period of this potential growth company?

Needed administrative people are given stock in lieu of salary. Cash is almost always tight in the early days of a new enterprise, and for a long time thereafter if growth is indeed rapid. Cash is needed to get people. People are needed to turn the wheels to make the cash flow. Add to those needs the enduring question of employee motivation and too often the answer comes up: Spread some stock around. It's a bad answer.

Here are a few of the reasons why. Stock can get into the hands of people you later have to fire. Stock can get into the hands of people who are unacceptable equity partners to investors you could otherwise attract for later rounds of financing. Stock spread around may well come back to the company (usually to the board of directors) on a repurchase option at exactly the point in time when the company can least afford to buy it, such as when the company or the economy is in a dip. And a few shares on the loose almost always end up in competitors' hands, giving them access to your quarterly or annual reports.

Does this mean that there is no room at all for stock or options for administrative people involved in a startup operation? The best answer is a qualified yes. Until the enterprise has some stability—has passed permanently beyond the point of negative cash flow, for instance—restrict the ownership risks and potential rewards to the primary participants who, by definition, are making a unique, direct contribution. And beyond the point of initial stability, issue stock to secondary company builders only after giving the matter deep, detailed, long-term thought. Stock certificates worth less than the buyer paid for them or those that are dropping in book value aren't exactly instruments of motivation.

The board of directors consists solely or primarily of insiders —company officers, their spouses, and friends. Legal matters aside, the operating purpose of a board is to aid, abet, challenge, and replace as necessary the chief executive officer (CEO) of the enterprise in pursuit of the stockholders' expressed interests. Those interests are generally financial (fiduciary) in nature, so a growth company board ideally concentrates on helping the CEO optimize the financial performance of the company over some finite period of time. If the CEO/entrepreneur is open to seasoned advice (see "creative conflict" above), he or she is unlikely to get it—or at least anything very powerful—from insiders, spouses, or friends. A properly constituted board can inexpensively double the width of a young company's management's point of view. One or two directors with the right experience base can add up to a sound primary participant. A strong board can be your single best source of the "right questions" mentioned earlier.

People with widely varying motives are mixed together in the same financial lifeboat. There was a day when professional investors liked to see the entrepreneurs they backed up to their beltlines in mortgages and other indebtedness to insure that they would keep their eyes on the till. Those days have generally passed, at least in the larger entrepreneuring areas of the country. But the principle still applies. Some people are vocationally after long-term capital gains; others are after a comfortable annual income; still others are primarily interested in professional challenge and its tributaries, problem solving, "expression," and, perhaps, fame. The smart entrepreneur will illuminate the driving force in each of his or her potential colleagues and think hard about whether there is compatibility across the basic team.

It is more than honorable for a group of talented people to join together to start a new company that aims to give each of them a chance to "do their thing" and, incidentally, make a buck in the process. Problems will arise, however, if responsible outside investors are brought in under the false pretenses that the management intends to grow, multiply, and make them (the investors) rich in a fixed number of years.

In summary, commandment one is important because a new company is a fragile thing. Like an egg shell, it is vulnerable to damage, if not destruction, from every direction. It needs a well-developed internal system of supports and braces to withstand the pressure of entering and competing successfully in a marketplace. Appropriate supports and braces can be conceived and squeezed into place by dedicated people with qualifications especially suited to the configuration of a particular egg. The entrepreneur faces the task of assimilating just the right number of right people. Too few results in weakness; too many in chaos; and wrong ones produce dissension.

2

The Second Commandment

Define the business of the enterprise in terms of what is to be bought, precisely by whom, and why.

Businesses are organs of society that perform tasks associated with providing most goods and services the public decides it wishes to own and use. Under this capitalistic system, a business can prosper to the extent it performs its particular tasks effectively and efficiently within the law. The nature of the tasks to be performed usually changes over time as those served change. The successful company predicts and responds to its chosen customers' needs. Customers, therefore, define the business. At all times, some customers are growing in their ability to buy; others are declining. The astute manager ascertains which is which.

Over twenty years ago, Ted Levitt published an article entitled *Marketing Myopia*, which is still influencing the way a lot of business people think about their world.* Levitt pointed out that customers buy need satisfactions, not products. He illustrated his point with two famous examples of business myopia. Why did the railroads of the nation—once very prosperous, growth businesses—fall from grace? Because railroad business people persisted too long in selling their product, rail-bound movement, and failed to recognize that customers were buying transportation. Transportation was the

* Theodore Levitt, "Marketing Myopia," *Harvard Business Review*, July–August, 1960, p. 45.

generic need being satisfied, and when new forms (airplanes, trucks, cars) came along, there was no reluctance among railroad customers to switch. Had railroad managements been less myopic, they would have led the way with new forms of transportation.

A similar story emanated from the movie industry. What were people buying when they went to the movies? The movie business people of the 1940s assumed the answer was movies, of course. Levitt noted that a more useful view would have been that people were buying entertainment. If movie people had focused on the generic need for entertainment, they would have been the first into television when it appeared.

Entrepreneurs face three related occupational hazards. First, they tend to concentrate too heavily upon what they have to sell and too lightly upon what is being bought—the myopia problem outlined above. This is a particularly prevalent hazard with engineers, scientists, and inventors who, almost by definition, are likely to be deeply intertwined with their product or process. Second, entrepreneurs tend to generalize about who the real customers are. "Companies" and "consumers" are extremely large classes of potential buyers. Finally, entrepreneurs in their enthusiasm and infectious optimism sometimes fail to pinpoint the reasons why a given, individual decision maker might buy the entrepreneur's specific new product, service, or experience. "Because it's better," lacks something in terms of precision.

Following are three short cases to illuminate these hazards to a successful startup operation.

CASE C. Two technical (electromechanical) people left a major west coast instrument manufacturer to cofound a teaching machine company. The product, an audiovisual-response device, worked well and seemed to have a number of potential applications. Consider the dictates of commandment two and think about these three questions.

1. What might customers buy from the new company?
2. Who might make the buying decisions?
3. Why might various types of buyers buy the teaching machine?

—Think about the answers before proceeding.—

Here is a partial list of possible answers to the questions.

1. Customers might buy teaching machines to:

Reduce teacher or instructor costs
Improve student or trainee retention of material
Increase efficiency (more people taught per teacher hour)
Improve utilization of facilities
Help slow learners

2. The buying decision might be made by:

Academic Market Segment
   Teachers
   School administrators
   School boards
   PTAs
Business/Industrial Market Segment
   Profit center managers
   Training directors
   Personnel managers
   Purchasing agents

3. A given buyer might buy to:

Improve his or her performance
Enhance his or her reputation as an innovator
Capture available investment tax credits before they expire
Experiment
Avoid hiring additional people

There are a lot of possibilities! Effective entrepreneuring requires that the possibilities be reduced in number to the point where "rifle shot" marketing becomes possible.

> CASE D. A famous tennis champion started a chain of tennis camps. Initially he had summer camps for children. Then he began expanding to week-long and weekend programs for adults. Essentially the same marketing, advertising, and operations approach was used for both segments of the tennis camp market. The venture into the adult market failed. Commandment two was violated.

	Children Camps	Adult Camps
What is bought?	1. Tennis skills	1. Social mixing
	2. Camp experience	2. Vacation
	3. "Baby" sitting service	3. Tennis skills
Who buys?	Parents	Adults—mostly singles
Why?	1. Child development	1. New experience
	2. Social status	2. Physical fitness
	3. Free up time during school vacation	3. Athletic prowess
		4. Meet opposite sex

In this instance, properly defining the business in terms of its customers could only lead to the conclusion that, in fact, there were at least two tennis businesses. Each business had its own distinct marketing and operations requirements for success.

> **CASE E.** Several physicians teamed up to take advantage of the opportunity they saw to use computers in hospitals. They pulled together an extraordinarily sharp group of programmers and systems people and developed packages for a variety of applications. The physician/entrepreneurs produced a large, handsomely-bound business plan. One seasoned investor made these notes on the cover after a detailed reading of the plan:
>
> "I can't tell if you are intending to sell a) time savings to the doctors, b) fewer nurses per floor or ward to the hospital administrators, c) greater revenue to the accounting people due to tighter controls on miscellaneous changes, or d) shorter hospital stays to patients and insurance companies."
>
> The potential investor said "no" to the investment opportunity.

Of course, if an entrepreneuring team such as the one in Case E has enough money, it may be able to muddle through the range of alternatives and eventually ferret out one or more solid, profit-making opportunities. There is almost always going to be some muddling, which is why a young company needs an adequate supply of money ("capitalization") up front. But there is a lot to be said for minimizing the muddle factor beforehand with hard thought, market research, field interviews, etc. Up to some point short of paralysis by analysis, the prospective enterprise should be defined as tightly as possible on paper. This doesn't preclude deviations in direction based on new information later on. It may, however, help you avoid spending a lot of energy and money only to find that "there's no there, there."

> **CASE F.** An adult student and later friend of the tennis champion in Case D above conceived and developed a videotape device. It was designed to allow tennis pros (and perhaps ski school pros) to record students' motions and play them back with stop action and other diagnostic features. The engineer/entrepreneur, the champ, and everyone who saw themselves played back on the screen bubbled with enthusiasm. Money was raised (easily) for a new venture based on the device and production was inaugurated amid appropriate fanfare. (After all, how could a champ be wrong?) The company expected to sell 1000-2000 units at around $4000 each the first year—a projection based weakly on selling units to only a "reasonable" percentage of the number of teaching pros, racquet clubs, etc., across the country. The fledgling company sold a grand total of twenty-three units nationwide during its first year in business.

What went wrong? Very simple. Tennis pros generally saw (and see) themselves as artists. They didn't "need" diagnostic devices, particularly ones that were cumbersome and required maintenance. In addition, many of them didn't care much for the champ who was featured in the advertisements. And finally, neither the teaching pros nor the clubs that provided the courts had much spending money.

The world of interest to the entrepreneur is filled with individuals who have some amount of change in their (or their companies') pockets. The most basic business transaction occurs when an individual exchanges his or her change for whatever it is you are selling. If there are enough individuals willing to make that exchange at a price that allows you to reach and persuade them, pay your way, and have enough left over to make the effort and risk worthwhile, then you may have a case for proceeding with a new enterprise. Otherwise, don't. If you are unsure, tiptoe until you can assemble enough hard data from customers (purchase orders, letters of intent, survey results, field tests) to justify a "go" decision. Getting balanced input from others qualified to entrepreneur with you (commandment one) and agonizing through the preparation of a business plan (commandment four) can help you sort through and rationalize the maze of options that confront the top people in a new enterprise.

3

The Third Commandment

> Concentrate all available resources on accomplishing two or three specific, operational objectives within a given time period.

Enterprises have finite resources. A smaller company achieves competitive advantage when playing for limited, explicit gains in a marketplace of its own choosing. Specialization breeds an organization sensitive to opportunities and quick to act. But any advantage withers if follow-through is weak. It will be weak if resources are dissipated. Resource dilution is a sure formula for mediocrity, a state of being that aspiring growth businesses cannot afford.

MBO (Managing by Objectives) has been a popular phrase since the 1960s when the acronym and practice was gradually assimilated into the inventory of management techniques. In effect, when working with objectives, an entrepreneur or manager determines what he or she wants to accomplish, by when, and sets out to reach that objective. The individual involved focuses on the end result and tries to make it happen. The alternative, working without objectives, causes an individual to focus on day-to-day activities, to work hard, and hope everything turns out all right.

There are four major variations on how to manage a business without using objectives.

Managing by Extrapolation (MBE)*

Users of this system keep on doing what they have always done. More is normally merrier, and over time all lines on the planning chart move upward and to the right. This essentially historical approach was adequate during the first half of this century because of the latent demand for products and services as the population in the United States grew in size and nature from a largely rural society to an almost completely urban one. Car companies and their suppliers produced and distributed cars; radio companies made radios; banks handled money; and so forth. Even after World War II, business was in a relatively steady state in which tomorrow could be reasonably expected to look a lot like yesterday. The primary task for top managers was to do the same things right—that is, more efficiently. A look at the national productivity curve during the 1950s and 1960s shows that, in total, business managements succeeded in doing things right. In more recent times, attention has been shifted to doing the right things through activities such as strategic planning.

Managing by Crisis (MBC)

This system, long the specialty of the entrepreneur, has picked up a larger following in recent times for two reasons. First, business life is much more complex than it used to be. Thus there are more crises to be handled. Second, there are a great many more engineers in positions of management responsibility today. As a group they tend to be great problem solvers. Give them a crisis and they will smother it with energy and innovation. Should there be a gap in the flow of problems, chances are good that one can be invented—something nice and tangible that a manager can get his or her arms around, or teeth into. Management by crisis is popular.

* Steven C. Brandt, *Strategic Planning in Emerging Companies* (Reading, Mass.: Addison-Wesley, 1981), pp. 11–14.

At the end of any given day, no one can say the boss didn't earn his or her pay.

Managing by Subjectives (MBS)

As the cat said to Alice as she hesitated along the path to Wonderland, if you don't know where you are going, any road will take you there. There are companies that operate successfully this way. Everyone does the best he or she can to accomplish what he or she thinks should be done. Somewhere up in the organization there is presumed to be a guiding star. And there could well be. As long as the business lends itself to masterminding (or central processing) by a single individual or a small team, implementation is relatively straightforward and not much talent is needed below the top level. The mystery approach to where a company is headed can work as long as the business is simple. For an emerging company, however, the days are numbered for such an approach to managing.

One of the prices of rising from obscurity to visibility is that the dynamic company becomes the object of the attention of various consumer activists, government agencies, stockholders, analysts, and the press. Who is the company hiring? Who is it trying to hire? Who is it firing? Why? Where is it headed? What are the projections? How big is the market share? What is the trend? And so on. "No comment" is an unacceptable answer. A dictionary definition of the word "subjective" is:

. . . *existing or originating within the observer's mind or sense organs and, hence, incapable of being checked externally or being verified by other persons.*

A subjective approach to employees' concerned questions—Where are we headed? How are we doing? How am I doing?—is unlikely to attract and hold the caliber of people required to capitalize on a competitive advantage. Few new enterprises do more than one thing really well. The presence of a continuing and overriding business objective can serve as a rallying point, if people know what it is.

Managing by Hope (MBH)

Most readers over forty years old recognize that the pace of living in the corporate world has increased markedly in recent years. Every business decision, such as staffing, capital investment, and new services, has more ramifications than before. Certainties are hard to find. The uncertainties of the times have led some managements into willy-nilly diversification in the hope that going in all directions at once will work out. The same uncertainties have led other managements into paralysis by analysis while they hope something will turn up to point the way for the enterprise. MBH is, essentially, a form of reacting rather than acting, of letting events control management rather than vice versa. It is the other end of the spectrum from MBO.

For those serious about entrepreneuring, a sound operational objective is one that is measurable, dated, and critical as a stepping stone at a given point in time. For example, for any given week or month or quarter or year, objectives can be formulated in the areas of profitability, cash flow, staffing, product development, production, sales volume, and so forth. Business judgment based on a combination of facts, advice, and intuition should guide those on the entrepreneuring trail to the proper areas to choose for setting objectives. Creative conflict among the primary participants should lead to agreement on the measures and dates and probably the accountability of who (specific name) "owns" each objective set.

Exercise

PART I.

Picture a startup company in which three cofounders have left their previous jobs, scraped together $50,000 from personal sources, and spent four months working day and night designing a new device that they think will revolutionize the way paper labels are applied to cans and bottles by food and beverage companies. As the trio completes its fourth month, the product prototype clearly works in the shop (a garage, naturally). At a Saturday morning meeting the entrepreneurs congratulate themselves on coming so far ("We did it!"). They then properly turn their thoughts to, "What next?" A number of areas in which objectives could be set are discussed. Some possible objectives are formulated and listed on a four-by-eight-foot piece of plywood which has the company name, Widgetronics, Inc., carefully lettered across the top.

Please examine that list, shown below, and decide *which of the ten "objectives" are sound in the way they are stated.*

	SOUND? (√)	
	YES	NO
1. Field test the prototype.	———	———
2. Obtain some orders.	———	———
3. Prepare a business plan.	———	———
4. Identify, interview, and hire a bookkeeper.	———	———
5. Line up money by end of quarter.	———	———
6. Get minimum of 1000 full-load hours on each of three devices by September 30. (Keep detailed maintenance log.)	———	———
7. Obtain two firm purchase orders for trial installations by October 31.	———	———
8. Draft a twelve-month plan and submit to Board by August 15.	———	———
9. Add a part-time bookkeeper no later than end of quarter.	———	———
10. Contact enough potential investors before September board meeting to find at least three interested in Widgetronics.	———	———

To repeat an earlier statement, for a new enterprise a sound objective is one that is measurable, dated, and critical at that point in time. How many objectives were sound as stated?

Given our criteria, only the last five of the above objectives were sound. The first five were pleasant statements of good intentions or ideas. Numbers six through ten, however, have some bite and lend themselves to accountability. By September 30 did _____ (someone's name) get a minimum of 1000 full-load hours on each of three machines? With such an objective, someone can succeed or fail, be rewarded or reprimanded, and keep his or her eye on the right "ball." When an entrepreneuring team has a small, *coordinated* set of smart objectives, the chances of moving a company successfully from nothing to something are vastly improved.

What are "smart" objectives?

Exercise

PART II.

Here are objectives numbered six through ten from the list above:

6. Get minimum of 1000 full-load hours on each of three devices by September 30. (Keep detailed maintenance log.)
7. Obtain two firm purchase orders for trial installations by October 31.
8. Draft a twelve-month plan and submit to Board by August 15.
9. Add a part time bookkeeper no later than end of quarter.
10. Contact enough potential investors before September board meeting to find at least three interested in Widgetronics.

Assume it is early August and you are advising the Widgetronics founders on what they should concentrate on next. Further assume that for some good and sufficient reason the Widgetronic management team has decided it will only "formally" adopt a maximum of two operational objectives for the next phase of the business. Which two of the six would you recommend?

Hard to say, isn't it? From the limited information avail-

able to you on Widgetronics it is very difficult to decide what
is most critical to the health of the enterprise in the fourth
month of its first year. Arguments can be advanced for completing the product testing, getting a solid order or two, laying out a plan, adding staff to keep the paperwork in order,
and cultivating investors. There will also always be a compelling argument for doing everything at once! Doing (or trying
to do) everything at once is a common failing of entrepreneurs. The only practical safeguard is the active presence
of one or two primary participants with the desired proclivity
for managing with objectives. As stated in the exposition immediately following commandment three at the start of this
chapter, "Resource dilution is a sure formula for mediocrity."

Why only two senior objectives for Widgetronics? There's
nothing magic about two, or one, or three—one per founder.
The point is that it should be a small number. When everybody does everything, nothing gets done well. The antithesis
is when everyone concentrates on just one or two prime
results. There's normally room for getting some other things
done too. The task is to make sure the other things don't de-
tract from accomplishing the main things.

There are many distractions in entrepreneuring. For example, there are a lot of fun things to do such as design letter-
heads, pick out offices, visit the printer, and drop by the
bank. There are a lot of satisfying and comfortable things to
do too, comfortable in that you have done them well in the
past. For example, you may feel real good about product engineering, working in the plant, selling, hustling investors, or
whatever. It's easy to use up the lion's share of your time doing what you do best, regardless of the most pressing needs of
the business. And then there are the "interesting" new challenges such as producing quality goods without the right
tools; cold-calling on potential customers who have never
heard of you, your company, or your spectacular new service; phoning a venture capitalist for the umpteenth time to
see if he or she has even read your business plan yet; and
taking prospective key employees to dinner with your own
money. How does an effective entrepreneur go about making
the right trade-off decisions between the different calls on his
or her finite time? There's no formula, but experience indicates that the omnipresence of crisp, agreed-upon objectives
helps.

4

The Fourth Commandment

Prepare and work from a written plan that
delineates who in the total organization is
to do what, by when.

---

*Until committed to paper, intentions are seeds without soil,
sails without wind, mere wishes which render communication
within an organization inefficient, understanding uncertain,
feedback inaccurate, and execution sporadic. Without execution, there is no payoff. The process of committing plans to
paper is easy to postpone under the press of day-to-day
events. In the absence of a document, fully coordinated usage
of the resources of the business is unlikely. Each participant
travels along a different route toward a destination of his or
her own choosing. Decisions are made independently, without a map. Time is lost; energy squandered.*

"Getting it down on paper seemed to help," properly cap-
tures the verdict that many, if not most, successful entrepreneurs reach after they have toiled through the process of
preparing a business plan either for a new business startup or
for, say, the coming year in an ongoing enterprise. Beforehand, however, it's number one on the procrastinator's parade
of hits. Why is this so? Most people can write well enough.
Why do they hesitate to commit to paper what is in their
heads?

The answer is complex, but it boils down to this. What is
consciously in an entrepreneur's head is not as complete, as
good, or as promising as he or she pretends it is. More often
than not it is a refrain regardless of the fact that the owner

represents it as a symphony. He or she has an image which is disguised orally as a finished painting. The process of getting an idea down on paper in a business plan format is typically a very creative one. It is not merely a matter of translation from head to paper, but of actually generating the complete original, typically a heavy undertaking. That's why subconsciously the brain whispers to itself, "Procrastinate; procrastinate." It knows that there's big work ahead! Developing a symphony from a refrain or a painting from an image isn't easy. Generating a written plan for a serious business venture is in the same league.

There are several popular misconceptions about the basic purpose of business plans, particularly those describing a brand new venture. Some people promote them as documents for raising money. Others see the plans as essentially legal boiler plates to provide entrepreneurs with "I told you so's" later on if things go sour for investors or employees who bought in. Still others stress the preparation of a plan as a rite of passage, a cleansing experience that tends to separate the real players from the spectators and camp followers. A perspective that includes all these but is philosophically of much greater use is that *a business plan is a blueprint for building a business.* Few readers would attempt even the addition of a room to their houses without a "picture" to work from. A business plan is a word picture of what the entrepreneurial dream is, why the dream can be economically viable for those involved, and how the construction will be carried out over time.

As discussed in detail below, a business plan is most usefully thought of as an internal, operating document, not a showpiece for raising money or satisfying attorneys. A sound business plan can be an important contributor to success whenever one, two, three, or more people wish to organize and synchronize a purposeful business effort over time in order to achieve specified results. Whether or not money is raised at all or via the plan, whether or not an attorney ever touches it, whether or not anyone but the writers ever read it, the investment in preparing the blueprint most often will have a high rate of return. This is true even, and perhaps especially, when as a result of the effort to put together a workable, believable plan, an idea is abandoned. Zero conception is better than a stillbirth.

Starting a new growth enterprise is normally a relatively high risk proposition. If the venture is successful, that is, economically viable in a projected length of time, everyone is happy. If the venture is unsuccessful, careers, money, reputations, spouses, good health, and even lives can be lost. Given the requisite personal drive of the leaders involved, the height of risk tends to be proportional to the presence of two prime ingredients: 1) the directly applicable experience and managing ability of the team responsible for the venture and 2) the thoroughness of the thinking that goes into the undertaking before it starts. To some extent, they are interchangeable.

Part of the folklore of venture capital is that it is most profitable over the longer haul to bet on good people rather than simply great concepts. "Back a quality individual before backing a surefire idea," said George Quist of Hambrecht and Quist, one of the oldest and most respected venture capital firms in the country. When pressed for what the indicators of good people or quality individuals are, most people experienced with evaluating entrepreneurs end up with a list that covers the following:

• Evidence of drive and achievement orientation
• Applicable (and successful) business and/or technical experience
• Verifiable integrity
• Ability to communicate ideas and plans

Increasingly, a fifth indicator is finding its way onto the list, namely a propensity toward team work. The turbulent times—current and projected—spawn complexity along every avenue of the business world. A variety of skills are needed to successfully cope with the myriad of issues that confront any growth company of consequence. No one individual is likely to have them all in sufficient depth to do a quality job on a sustaining basis. In short, one-person bands are falling from favor.

A final point of perspective and perhaps clarification is that by definition a prospectus is "a report or statement which describes or advertises a forthcoming literary work, a flotation of stock, etc." A prospectus is not a business plan. A business plan, however, may technically be a prospectus if it is used to raise money.

In summary, after preparing a business plan, the entrepreneurial management team involved should have before it an agreed program for action and results to which it will

willingly commit itself. After reading a business plan, a director, potential investor, or other interested party should know
precisely what those involved intend to do, by when, with the
human and financial resources called for in the plan.

Guide to Preparing a Business Plan

The length and sequence of contents in a business plan for a
startup will vary somewhat depending upon the complexity of
the proposed venture. A few key elements are almost always
needed, however, to describe just why, how, and when
economic viability will be accomplished. While other objectives may exist and even be of greater importance to the
writers of a given plan, economic viability is the one necessary condition around which the contents outlined below are
molded. Without economic viability, few business ventures,
no matter how noble, survive for long.

"Why" is normally addressed by first identifying precisely
who outside the enterprise is interested in and qualified to
buy whatever it is the enterprise will have to sell, the way it
will be sold. "How" is indicated by a complete coverage of
the human, production, organizational, and monetary requirements for providing the product or service on a timely and
continuing basis consistent with the pricing and quality demands of the chosen marketplace. "When" is reflected by a
thorough presentation of the financial implications over time
of each important event called for in the plan.

In a plan that is to be read critically by others, it is useful
to have an overview or executive summary at the start. Such
a section will presumably be written last even though it appears first. Overall, then, the contents of a basic blueprint for
building a business are as follows:

> Overview
> Concept
> Objectives
> Market Analysis
> Production
> Marketing
> Organization and People

Funds Flow and Financial Projections
Ownership

1.0 CONCEPT

As suggested earlier, there is powerful evidence that the act of committing an idea to paper is a vital step in its development. This is nowhere more true than when dealing with the fundamental idea underlying the formation of a new, growth venture. By nature, new ideas are fuzzy combinations of needs, interests, capabilities, frustration, optimism, ambition, and a dozen other ingredients. Few entrepreneurs wake up one morning with an "ah ha" imprinted undeniably on their brains. Instant photography, fail-safe computers, resoleable tennis shoes, hang gliders, fast food stores, and microcomputers were not conceived with the help of lightning bolts.

In most instances, a notion or inkling takes some encouragement before it becomes a hunch. A hunch requires some massaging and mulling before it graduates into a discussion piece. A discussion piece demands conversation and research enroute to precarious classification as a full blown idea. And an idea takes work, work, work to refine it into a concept upon which to found a business.

With a single, well-developed concept, a massive business empire can be built. But a single product or service is seldom enough to justify the bodily wear and tear required to launch a business intended for the Fortune 500.

Here are a few examples to illustrate the difference between a product or service and at least one possible underlying concept.

Product/Service	*Possible Concept*
Quick hamburgers	Mass-produced restaurant food
Part-time secretarial help	Peak load, variable cost labor
Microcomputer software packages	Electronic publishing
Better mouse trap	Rodent control for homemakers
Inventory control for small auto parts retailers	Hardware/software packages for selected vertical markets

Solar pool heaters	Domestic energy transformation devices
Buggy whips (historic example!)	Transportation stimulators (!!)
Raw material control system for paper machines	Productivity improvements for process industries
Tennis shoe resoleing	Apparel recycling

The listing above does contain a touch of tongue in cheek. It is extremely unlikely that all the entrepreneurs responsible for the various products and services shown initially elevated their basic ideas to the conceptual level. The question is whether or not it would have been valuable for them to think the implications of their product or service all the way through to the customer/generic level sooner rather than later (as outlined in commandment two).

There is another compelling reason to hammer a concept out in black and white. The possibility of confusion, misunderstanding, and shallowness on the issue of what business we are in is reduced. A reasonably refined concept can help insure that the second product or service of a budding enterprise is synergistic and complementary to the first.

> **CASE G.** Engineer Ed came up with a new machine that sorted bad peanuts from good peanuts on a high-volume basis. He founded a manufacturing company that did very well for himself and two investors. Based on his initial success, Ed was able to attract a sizeable amount of investment money to keep on building the business. He expanded into the distribution of irradiated plastics—a field completely foreign to his early peanut machine manufacturing and sales success. Ed's company peaked out at a modest size.

Make no misunderstanding. Ed did all right for himself financially. But he never built the big company of his dreams. Ed's eclectic, opportunistic approach has its place. So does making a big splash with a single product and then selling the embryonic company to a bigger company interested in expanding its product line. Take the money and run! Or start over again. It's a matter of what the founders are out to accomplish (commandment one). If you and your associates are out to build a major business, time invested in identifying and refining your concept can have a big payoff.

2.0 OBJECTIVES

The third commandment, covered earlier, stressed the importance and characteristics of sound objectives. Two levels of objectives should be included in a business plan. First, the longer-term interests ("intentions," "objectives") of the entrepreneur(s) should be identified. Second, the operating objectives—sales, profits, market share, margins—need to be spelled out. Both levels typically require a great deal of digging.

What do the plan writers hope to achieve for themselves over the longer term? Most everybody, at a minimum, wants to make at least enough money to get along. But there is a huge difference in pursuing $1,000,000 in capital gains within three years and pursuing a steady stream of $60,000 net income per year for life. Neither of these two extremes holds the corner on virtue vis-à-vis the other, but they *are* different. And knowing roughly what you, the plan writer(s), are after is important. Otherwise, critical readers of the plan don't know against what to measure its validity.

> **CASE H.** Sandra and Kay came up with an idea for a one-stop-shopping phone service for prepriced, guaranteed, home repair work. In concept, it was sort of a AAA for home owners in newer sub-divisions where people in need of a plumber, electrician, or a tree surgeon tended to have only the yellow pages for guidance.
>
> The two women spent many hours fleshing out the idea. A thousand questionnaires were mailed to a randomly-selected cross section of the residents in burgeoning Contra Costra County near San Francisco. More than 10 percent of the questionnaires were answered and returned. The answers were encouraging, and the entrepreneurs wisely cross-checked the results with a variety of potential users, suppliers, and community-knowledgeable acquaintances. The end result of the research phase was the finding that the business idea appeared to be capable of supporting one, maybe two, people (owner/managers) modestly.
>
> Is the idea a good one? Should the women proceed?

It depends. This is a good example of why it is important for an entrepreneur to know his or her personal objective(s). If Sandra and/or Kay were considering entrepreneuring to get rich, this home repair idea probably was not the way to do it. If they wanted to serve mankind or occupy their time while earning a living, it had some possibilities.

Perhaps the biggest mistake to avoid, however, would be for Sandra and Kay to launch into the business with the question of personal objectives unexamined. It's an everyday occurrence to find business partnerships and young corporations on the rocks because the participants found out "later" that one of them wanted to reinvest earnings and expand the business while the other preferred to take his or her share of the profits and spend it on long vacations in Europe! Proceeding with a new enterprise with people who have mixed motives is what keeps attorneys in Mercedes Benzes.

Personal objectives come in all shapes and colors. There

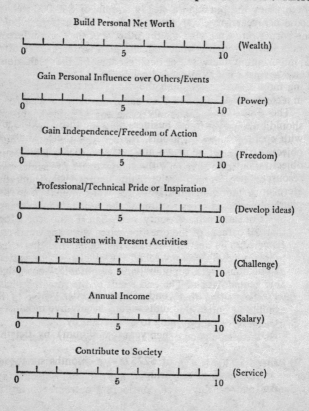

Build Personal Net Worth

0   5   10   (Wealth)

Gain Personal Influence over Others/Events

0   5   10   (Power)

Gain Independence/Freedom of Action

0   5   10   (Freedom)

Professional/Technical Pride or Inspiration

0   5   10   (Develop ideas)

Frustation with Present Activities

0   5   10   (Challenge)

Annual Income

0   5   10   (Salary)

Contribute to Society

0   5   10   (Service)

seem to be seven important scales along which potential starters of businesses might usefully calibrate themselves.

Why are *you* interested in building a new company? Circle a number that corresponds to your personal level of motivation. Ten is high.

These seven scales are not meant to be exhaustive or definitive. Ten points is not necessarily good on a given scale. There have been hundreds of studies of whether successful entrepreneurs are born or made, renegades (from society) or heroes, lucky or inspired, identifiable in advance or random marriages of opportunity and capability. There's a small school of thought in favor of each point of view, and chances are that the points of view will proliferate in the last part of this century as more pet rock syndromes flash across the horizon. The seven scales above used as points of departure, however, can help an entrepreneur be honest with himself or herself and with the other contributors to the business plan—the blueprint for building the business. One thing is for certain. A business plan written by people with widely-differing or conflicting personal objectives is likely to end up looking more like a camel than the thoroughbred needed to win in a competitive industry.

The second and more obvious level of objectives that should be included in the business plan are those having to do with operations—sales, profits, market share, etc. The word, objective, implies "what we are going to make happen." An objective is more than a wish. It is an *end result* to which resources—cash and people—will be allocated to produce. Here are some objectives lifted from a variety of business plans.

$100,000,000 in sales by 1990.

Market share of 3 percent by end of third year.

Ninety systems installed and working by 1985.

Four thousand billable hours by the twenty-fourth month of operations.

Positive cash flow by end of first calendar year.

Shipments of 25,000 units within twenty-five months.

Gross margins declining to 40 percent by. . . .

ROE of 35 percent per year (minimum) by the third year.

Profit (before tax) of $225,000 in months six through eighteen after startup.

And so on.

In short, objectives define the nature and perimeter of the business you are planning to build by a specified point in time. Some operating objectives will change from year to year, of course, as certain milestones are passed and new subjects rise in importance. As objectives change so must the supporting business plan change. The fourth commandment is always with you! Prepare and work from a written plan year after year.

There are two trends occurring in the nature of operating objectives as the 1980s skip by. One is that there is an increasing interest across the land in such measures as ROI (Return on Investment) and ROE (Return on Equity). In these times, it is less and less adequate to state merely how you are doing or how you expect to do in a profit and loss sense. Nowadays the question is more and more how you expect to do with the resources or assets at your disposal. This is more of a balance sheet orientation.

For example, which company is doing better, X or Y?

	Company X	Company Y
Sales Last Year	$20,000,000	$30,000,000
Sales Growth over Previous Year	50%	20%
Profit percentage on Sales	15%	5%
Market Position	Strong	Strong

Which company is doing "better"?

Would you answer be the same if you knew that the total assets (debt and equity) in company X were $10,000,000 and the total assets in company Y were $5,000,000?

Would your answer be different again if you knew that the equity in X was $3,000,000; in Y, $1,000,000? Think about it.

Obviously, which company is doing better—based on the data given—depends on your criteria. Entrepreneurs are increasingly being confronted with the issue of the "quality" of the growth they are projecting. Quality typically is based on a comparison. Upon what asset or equity base are the projected sales or earnings constructed? Overall, asset *productivity* is another way to think about the challenge facing modern day managers who must number fluctuating interest rates, inflation, OPEC gyrations, and certain kinds of employee shortages among the ingredients in building their businesses. The use of objectives (measurable, end results to be achieved) has become increasingly important as one of the few antidotes to complexity and confusion in these turbulent times.

Henry David Thoreau said once, "In the long run, men hit only what they aim at." A business plan needs to be "aimed at" something that is responsive to both the plan writers' personal interests and the known, basic requirements for success as an economic entity in the chosen marketplace and arena of competition.

3.0 MARKET ANALYSIS

There's a difference between a need and a market. To use a classic example, the management of Ford Motor Company at one point in time perceived a need for a large, flashy car with a lot of gadgetry in the "cockpit." They gave the world the Edsel automobile. For a variety of reasons, the perceived need was not a reality when the car was introduced. There was only a very limited *market*, namely people favorably disposed toward buying a large, flashy, futuristic car.

Here is another example. For some years now a few manufacturers have been cultivating, even titillating a need for video disc players in the home. The same is going on today with personal computers. The cultivating is slowly paying off, and gradually the perceived "need" is being converted around the edges into a market—once again, people favorably disposed toward buying the product. The purpose of the *market* analysis section of a business plan is to identify as precisely as possible the size, location, and characteristics of the set of people who are expected to be favorably disposed toward buying what the new enterprise expects to sell.

Please note with care the contents of the last sentence. It includes ". . . people . . . favorably disposed toward buying. . . ." If you are planning to get money in the form of sales dollars from people not yet "favorably disposed" toward your new product or service, then it is important that you state as much in your market analysis. There's nothing categorically wrong with undertaking to create a market. Many, many entrepreneurs have done it. Doing so requires what is appropriately called missionary marketing. But it's expensive, and your capitalization will have to be sufficient to cover it.

CASE I. The energy crunch of 1974 spawned a number

of solar products companies. One of the more exciting ones had a swimming pool heating system based on some technologically-advanced collector panels. The need for saving pool heating dollars via solar energy seemed obvious enough. The founder had to decide if there was a market. If so, could that market be reached cost-effectively?

Extensive field work indicated that there was a market within a certain product price range. But, having identified a market, it turned out that there was no straightforward way to sell to and service it. The founder faced the hard choice of abandoning his idea or assembling a distribution system from scratch. He raised enough money to do the latter.

Once isolated, the total population of all potential buyers—consumers or corporate representatives such as purchasing agents, officers, or department heads—for a given product or service is a certain size. Call it X. Within X there are discrete subgroups called segments that vary in characteristics such as the reason for buying, financial ability to pay, and ease of reaching. Most new enterprises need to select a segment or a very limited number of segments upon which to concentrate available selling efforts. In the market analysis section of your business plan, you are interested primarily in describing the magnitude and nature of the business opportunity. Later sections deal with how you expect to pursue the opportunity in the chosen segment(s).

What are the characteristics of markets that are attractive "bets" to growth company investors? A very rough outline of the criteria used by a cross section of west coast venture capitalists is as follows. The targeted market should be:

- Over $50,000,000 in total size (annual sales volume).
- Growing at a rate significantly greater than the real GNP.
- Sufficiently fragmented or noncompetitive to allow an aggressive new entry to grow to $25,000,000 or more in sales within five years.
- Amenable to profit making by a new entry at a rate of at least 5 to 10 percent (after tax) on sales within two to three years after startup.
- Socially and politically acceptable to the business world in general so that:

a. Traditional forms of financing such as bank loans are available to the company once it is established.
b. Sale of stock to the public or a larger corporation at a fair price is possible at a later point in time.

This outline is, as stated, rough. There is a lot of art in making venture investments. Often the precise size of the market is not definable—at least to where it can be shown to be $50,000,000 or more. If a market is currently only $10,000,000 in size but it is predicted to grow at 50 percent a year for ten years, there may be plenty of room for a new entry. The overriding issue is whether there appear to be enough available sales dollars to support the proposed new enterprise over a reasonable length of time so that it can, in fact, develop a track record as a growth company.

One other point of great importance bears repeating. There are many good and proper reasons for entrepreneuring. Running a company up in size and selling out for a healthy capital gain is only one of them. But whatever the reason, an appropriate market must exist or be developed to satisfy the top line requirements dictated by the objectives of the primary participants. If there is an inadequate top line, there will be a poor bottom line. More on this in commandment seven.

Once the plan writer(s) have developed a comprehensive picture of the market to be pursued, the supporting or amplifying elements are relatively straightforward.

- What or who are any intermediate influences on the ultimate buyers? For example, will you have to work through dealers, distributors, sales representatives, associations, purchasing agents, or retailers? What hurdles or opportunities do they present?
- What are the existing and anticipated competitive conditions? How will they affect pricing, hiring, packaging, facility location, and transportation?
- Are there important governmental influences in the chosen market, such as those affecting the five E's: energy, equality, ethics, environment, and employment practices?

Where does one obtain market data? The list of sources is infinitely long. Appendix A contains a handy note used at the Harvard Business School that at least indicates the scope of possibilities for developing a picture of an industry or market opportunity. Ideally, one or more members on the entrepreneuring team has in-depth experience in the market to begin with. If not, triple the importance of this section of your business plan!

In summary, no one should try harder to understand the dynamics of the targeted marketplace than the potential "new kid on the block." Ultimately, business success flows from satisfying customers (commandment two).

4.0 PRODUCTION

There are a variety of ways to make most products. The mix between capital equipment and labor, made parts and bought parts, assemble here versus assemble there, and so forth has to be determined. Every decision has implications to product delivery times, cash flow, quality control requirements, and other elements of a manufacturing business such as staffing and facility requirements. Likewise, service business managements face early choices which often set a new business on a course from which it may be quite hard to turn later. Location is frequently a major consideration if customers need direct access to the business. People, high skill or low, must be available nearby or via their "electronic cottages," as described in Toffler's *The Third Wave*.* You can't produce custom wood furniture without skilled woodworkers, for example. Thus given a positive point of view about an identified market opportunity, producing to capitalize on that opportunity is a key blueprint ingredient.

Production plans probably flow easiest from hard to soft, that is, from equipment lists to systems considerations and people, once a production philosophy has been established. Production philosophies generally start with a decision about where the new company will position itself in the make versus buy syndrome. Two well-known, high-flying, publicly-held computer companies have each exceeded $80,000,000 in sales in recent years. Neither actually manufactures more than about 15 percent of its own hardware. Eighty-five percent of every system shipped consists of vendor supplied parts. This ratio is neither good nor bad, only different from the more

* Alvin Toffler, *The Third Wave* (New York: Bantam Books, 1981), p. 194.

traditional pattern of making what you sell. The ratio merely reflects what two different management teams have decided is best for their own enterprises.

What is best for your particular enterprise? There's no clean answer. It depends most on what it is your management team does best and where the money tends to get spent in your chosen industry. Take a look at the two examples below, A and B. A and B are not competitors. They are active in completely different industries and marketplaces. Both have distributions of costs that are near their respective industry averages.

	Allocation of One Dollar of Sales	
Company A		**Company B**
.08	Transportation	.15
.35	Distributor	
	Sales Representative	.10
.15	Internal Sales Force and Marketing	.10
.20	Cost of Goods Sold	.45
.22	Overhead, Research and Development, Profit	.20
$1.00		$1.00

More than half ($.58) of company A's dollar of revenue goes to moving the product after it is in inventory. Only $.20 is spent on cost of goods sold. Company B, on the other hand, spends $.45 on cost of goods sold. There is at least a preliminary argument that says that company A should allocate the bulk of its primary resources to nonmanufacturing matters if it is possible to do so. Company B management, in contrast, may wish to consider an opening production philosophy that leans more toward the manufacturing, assembly, or fabrication end of the continuum so they can whittle that $.45 down over time.

CASE J. In 1973 three men formed a new company with $250,000 of outside capital and a concept fashioned around user-friendly inventory control systems for selected market niches. The company, which was selling a $30,000 item to small proprietorships with annual sales typically under $1,000,000, was operating in the black after its second quarter in existence. It has been immensely profitable every quarter since, and today it enjoys sales exceeding $100,000,000 a year. It has also gone public and in 1981 maintained a price/earnings ratio of over thirty.

From its inception, the management has minimized the amount of manufacturing done in-house. Essentially all parts are purchased. Assembly work is even subcontracted to a variety of suppliers. "I didn't want for us to have to build big parking lots on expensive real estate," the president said. "Only the quality control work is done here. We have built our own staff in areas where we think we are experts—marketing, sales, and engineering. We're happy to let others [vendors] make a buck. They can take the ebb and flow of hiring and laying off production people too."

CASE K. A new bank was formed in a medium-sized metropolitan city with a population of 100,000. It was the only independent bank in the area. The founders were able to attract a sizeable block of opening capital. How should that capital be allocated (beyond buying a vault!)? A fancy building and offices? Staff? Computers and systems? Automated tellers? Marketing?

Some money had to go to each category, of course, but a carefully reasoned decision was made to put the lion's share into the staff rather than into buildings, marketing, or high speed production and processing systems, where no matter how much was spent, the new bank could not excel against competition. The founders did, however, go out and hire the premier people (from other banks, naturally) in the area.

The new bank exceeded its second year projections fifteen months after opening its modest doors for business.

What worked in Cases J and K are not formulas for you. The cases merely illustrate the point that a production philosophy needs to be thought through carefully before plans are made to spend money on real estate, bricks, mortar, or equipment. Peter Drucker points out in his book *Managing in Turbulent Times** that we are rapidly becoming a nation

* Peter F. Drucker, *Managing in Turbulent Times* (London: Pan Books Ltd., 1981), p. 26.

of knowledge workers. One manifestation of that trend is a change in the historic mix in how scarce resources are allocated between production, marketing, managing, and research and development activities.

Back to the business plan itself. Given a basic production philosophy, what then? It's time to get down to details.

- What processes are involved, and how will they be obtained?
- What equipment is needed to support or provoke efficient, in-house operations?
- Given the above, what are the facility requirements?
- What is the sourcing on raw materials, labor, supplies, and purchased parts? Who will oversee this sourcing in the company?
- How will incoming inspection, quality control, packaging, transportation, and repairs be managed?
- What is the schedule of who is to do what, by when, regarding production?
- From the above, what is the budget, the timing, and magnitude of expenditures?
- What will be done if the business grows much faster than expected? Or much, much slower?

As a general rule, the leaner a young enterprise is, the better. Money tied up in facilities, inventories, equipment, and other fixed costs reduces the ability of management to maneuver and adjust its plan and actions to changing conditions. At the same time, sufficient control over the production of the customer satisfaction being sold is important. The best marketing program in the world is a waste if the demand generated goes unsatisfied due to quality, cost, or delivery problems. Smart decisions allocating resources are one mark of managers who can excel in entrepreneuring.

5.0 MARKETING

As used here, marketing is a broad term that includes all aspects of creating customers. The business plan should reflect a detailed description of precisely how the targeted population described in the market analysis (section 3.0) will be allowed or coaxed to exchange its change for your product and/or service.

- What methods of selling and advertising are to be used? What will make the chosen channels of distribution productive—incentive systems, packaging innovations?
- What product or service features and benefits are to be emphasized?
  How do they stack up against competition?
- How is credit approval to be administered?
- Who is involved in pricing decisions, and what is the basis for those decisions—cost, value added, value to customer?
- What are the product or service development or evolution plans?
- What level, if any, of research and/or development activities are needed to sustain or accelerate the growth of business?
  [Note: Technology can be a separate and very large section of a total business plan, particularly for a technology-based venture. In such a section, the management team should spell out who and/or what will drive the needed development effort as well as what is expected to be accomplished, by when.]
- What competitive responses are anticipated, if any, and how will they be countered, if at all?
- What is the schedule of who is to do what, by when, regarding marketing?
- From the above, what is the budget, the timing, and magnitude of expenditures?
- What will be done if the business grows much faster than expected? Much, much slower than expected?

There is always an element of guesswork in predicting what is going to happen in the marketplace. This is one powerful reason why the width of management's experience base in the chosen industry is of prime importance to an outsider evaluating a proposed business. The broader the base, the more valid management's expectations should be and the less likelihood there is of surprises. Candidates for entrepreneuring who have backgrounds in the steel industry are going to be less than convincing when they describe their campaign to dominate the world yogurt market.

A final point of perspective under the general heading of marketing. You may have noted that the word strategy has not been used in this "Guide To Preparing A Business Plan." And it won't be used other than here because it is a word that has been overpublicized to the point of uselessness. Strategy can be defined as a summary statement of how objectives will be pursued. There can be manufacturing and financial strategies to achieve manufacturing and financial objectives, respectively. But there are fundamentally only six basic *corporate* strategies for building a business: product development, market development, forward integration, backward integration, diversification, and, of course, staying put, i.e., continuing to sell just what you have to your existing customers.

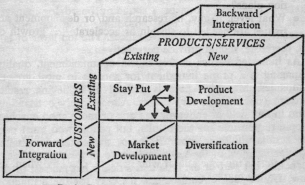

Basic Strategies for Building a Business

Ultimately, a statement of corporate strategy boils down to: To whom is the company going to sell what? This brings us back full circle to the more traditional label of marketing. In its broadest sense, marketing is the whole sector of interface between the new enterprise and the rest of the world. In just a few short years, a variety of now famous companies have shown just what can be achieved with smart marketing. Apple Computer, for example, has created satisfied customers in most every nook and cranny of the shrinking globe. Precisely the same kind of challenge faces the growth company entrepreneur.

6.0 ORGANIZATION AND PEOPLE

People make things happen. The right people make the right things happen. Selecting and fitting the right people to key responsibilities is a continuous process that ideally starts before or at the time the business plan is developed so that the document truly reflects the input of the team that is to execute it. There are at least four layers of talent potentially active in an enterprise: a board of directors or advisers, the general management, functional specialists, and other key individuals. Some people will contribute at more than one level.

As suggested in commandment one, directors are often chosen for convenience rather than for needed talents they might bring to the organization. This is a mistake. Qualified, interested, informed directors can be useful in guiding a company to economic viability. Properly used, a board can be an internal consulting group or a sounding board for management rather than just a legal appendage or a comfortable formality for the chief executive officer. The top layer of talent, therefore, should provide perspective.

As indicated earlier in this fourth commandment, quality managing is a prime ingredient for success in most growth companies. Managing here is defined as achieving results through (not with or for) others. Almost every outstanding team in any field of endeavor has one or more good coaches, people responsible for the results, but people who must pursue results via their subordinates or associates. In smaller companies, most of the key people have to wear a manager's (coach's) hat part of the time and a doer's hat the rest of the time. Under such circumstances, it's easy for the distinction between the two different kinds of work to become blurred.

Both kinds of work are necessary for success in entrepreneuring.

When blurring occurs, it is often the managing work that gets shoved aside in the rush of day-to-day pressures to get the orders, finish the design, and ship the orders, three examples of "doing" work. A proper organization will insure that managers are in place and motivated and allowed to spend the necessary time on planning and supervising others in pursuit of the goals of the enterprise.

CASE L. During the tennis boom of the mid-1970s a number of the major tennis stars of that era started tennis related businesses. One such business grew to several million dollars in sales from a diverse set of activities that included publishing, player managing, tennis camps, retail stores, and tournament promoting. The star-studded company lost money hand over fist. To reverse the loss, a CPA was hired to "fix the company." She installed the necessary control systems and helped get the company back to the point where it was at least breaking even. After successfully completing that Herculean task, she was made president. But no new accounting or control talent was added to pick up that phase of the rather complex operations. The CPA simply had two big jobs now instead of one. Within a year the company was deep in the red again, and the president was both "burned out" and fired.

What's the moral of the story? Just below the director or advisor layer of talent, there is a layer of management that must be provided for in the organization of a new venture if the founders wish to avoid having an *ad*venture on their hands. Most everyone who has been successful at doing something (selling, engineering, programming, accounting etc.) assumes he or she can also manage. *This is a faulty assumption.* More on this later in commandment five. Sound management is the second required layer of talent.

As a general rule, between the members of the management team and the board, the primary functional skills— marketing, production, accounting, finance, and technology (if appropriate)—should be well represented. Functional skills are the third layer of talent. It is not a problem if some functional skills are provided initially by board members (or possibly by consultants) rather than by full-time employees. This condition can be altered in time as the business grows. The important point for the entrepreneur is that he or she should not try to "fly on one wing" during the critical early days when there is a natural tendency to try to do everything yourself. If you want to build a growth company, get the money you need to get the people you need to do what the business must have done well to succeed in a mean, competitive environment. If you can't get the money you need, consider dropping or radically altering the idea. ("Retreat? Hell no! We're merely backing up to go around and try it another way.")

The fourth layer of talent in most embryonic organizations is the one that contains the one or two key individuals who possess the special talents indigenous to the specific business. A semiconductor company must have a solid-state physicist. A computer software company must have a senior programmer or two. Case L above was critically dependent upon tennis camp directors who could both play *and* manage. And a chocolate chip cookie company most likely needs a skilled baker somewhere in the organization. Sometimes the president or another officer is also the key technician. This works all right so long as the individual can keep his or her multiple jobs separate, straight, and well covered—either directly or via delegation.

What about organizational structure? Most new enterprises are going to start off with a functional structure—one level of general management, a president, with functional vice-presidents reporting to him or her.

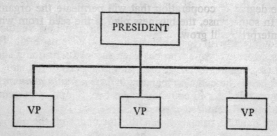

There are variations, of course. The vice-presidents can be responsible for products or geographic areas, for example, but usually such "profit center" structures with their multiple layers of general management make more sense later on. For a new company intent on growth, a simple functional organization with simple titles and an articulated policy of organizational flexibility over time is probably the best approach. In the business plan, then, the writers delineate the starting point. Later structures can then evolve over time with success.

Given the starting point, here are the major supporting details that can usefully be included under organization.

- Who is accountable to whom, and for what?
- What pay, incentives, benefits, and promotion sequences will be used to attract, stimulate, and hold desired people?
- How will salaries be determined and administered over time?
- When will various people (by job title) be added to the organization, over, say, the first year or so?
- From the above, what is the budget, the timing, and the magnitude of expenditures?

Capable people who understand what they are to accomplish and who are motivated to invest their energies in the enterprise are the basic building blocks the management team has. Increasing attention is being focused today on the people side of business. "Our perspective is that organizations are organic, not mechanical or hydraulic," say authors Pascale and Athos in their fine book *The Art of Japanese Management.* * The development of a positive, energetic corporate culture is best begun when the enterprise is small. The quality of the business planning effort itself is frequently a proper indicator of the degree of cooperation that will permeate the organization. In some sense, the business plan is the seed from which the enterprise will grow.

7.0 FUNDS FLOW AND FINANCIAL PROJECTION

Startup money (initial capitalization) is the mortar that holds the building blocks of a new growth company together until the merit of the company's product or service is widely enough recognized and valued in the marketplace to generate the earnings needed to continue the business. The amount and timing of the startup money needed is derived primarily from the production, marketing, organizational, and perhaps technology sections of the business plan discussed earlier.

New entrepreneurs often worry about how much of the company they will have to "give up" before they worry about how much mortar they need to successfully launch the enterprise. This is backward thinking. A healthier sequence of events goes like this: 1) Establish a frame of mind that says, "I'd rather own a smaller piece of a big pie than vice versa." 2) Recognize that you are not "giving up" anything, you are *selling* a piece of the company. 3) Solicit buyers (investors) if you require them, well prepared to negotiate the best possible price.

The price you are able to get for a portion of your company will depend on:

- How much money is needed
- The size of the opportunity (timing and size of the ROI)

---

* Richard Tanner Pascale and Anthony G. Athos, *The Art of Japanese Management* (New York: Simon and Schuster, 1981).

- The background of the management team
- The quality of the business plan
- The "chemistry" between the individuals
- What's going on in the world at the time of decision

It's academic to worry about "giving up an arm and a leg" matters until you have crystallized the size of the transaction. A detailed cash flow projection is the basic technique for determining the needs of a new business.

A cash flow projection consists of three fundamental elements: cash in, cash out, and timing. A skeleton projection looks like this:

Outline: Cash Flow Projection							
Periods		1	2	3	. . . . . .	N	TOTALS
Dates		Jan.	Feb.	Mar.			
Cash In							
a. Units Sold							
b. Units Shipped/Provided							
c. Price/Unit							
d. $ of Net Sales							
e. Sales $ Rec'd							
f. Discounts, Commissions Pd.							
g. Net Cash In							
Cash Out							
h. Cost of Goods Sold							
1. Purchases							
2. Materials							
3. Labor							
i. Management							
j. Marketing							
k. Administration							
l. Rent, Utilities, Phone							
m. Net Cash Out							
n. Cash Flow/Period							
o. Starting Cash							
p. Net Cash Flow							
q. Cumulative Cash Position							

Look first at the bottom line, q, labeled "Cumulative Cash Position." This is what the entrepreneur must ultimately keep his or her eye on. An enterprise cannot operate long with zero cash, and it certainly can't grow. In many respects, the cash flow projection is the summary road map of how you and your associates intend to build the new company. The cumulative cash position is your fuel gauge.

[One side comment: Today there are excellent cash flow projection programs (software) available quite inexpensively for microcomputers. By using such a program, prospective entrepreneurs can play "what if" with their cash flow planning without resorting to endless hours with pencils, erasers, and accounting paper.]

The periods at the top of the projection can be months, quarters, or years. Typically, the modern business plan will show months for the first year or two, quarters for an additional year or two, and years for the balance up to a total of four or five years. While few readers expect the later years projections to turn out to be 100 percent accurate, it is important that growth company founders think through their opportunity beyond a year or so, even if there are major unknowns.

Items a and b, "Units Sold" and "Units Shipped/Provided" are increasingly important indicators of the reasonableness of a given plan. (The units can be units of service, contracts, boxes of product, gallons—whatever is the basic element of transaction in the business.) If the rate at which units move is suspect, the validity of the entire cash flow will be open to question.

Picture this. Four people conceived an idea for a new company and prepared the following as part of their cash flow projection.

Cash in	Year 1	Year 2	Year 3
Units Sold	1000	2,300,000	9,000,000
Units Shipped	1000	2,000,000	8,000,000

How would you evaluate the figures shown? (√)	YES	NO
a. Looks like an exciting growth opportunity.	_____	_____
b. The year-to-year increases are quite sizeable, particularly between year one and year two.	_____	_____
c. The management will have to know a lot about marketing and production.	_____	_____

Of course, it's hard to make a determination without knowing what makes up the units. If the units are toothpicks, one conclusion might be reached. If the units are aluminum wheelbarrels, another conclusion. Regardless of the units, however, choice b is true, and probably so is choice c. Any business that is going to increase output by 2000 times over a twenty-four-month period (Year 1 & 2) has its work cut out for it! Optimism is important in entrepreneuring, alongside realism.

Returning to the outline, items c through m are straightforward. For a complicated business, for example one with a lot of engineering or a complex overhead structure, the number of line items included in the cash in and cash out calculations could number 100 or more. The important thing is to identify all significant cash sources and uses. Doing so will reduce (not eliminate) downstream surprises.

Item n is item g minus item m. The cash flow/period is the actual cash in hand at the end of the particular month, quarter, or year. [Note: the difference between items d and e is that d is the figure for invoices mailed; e is the cash actually received from customers. If your customers take sixty days to pay you, there's a sixty day lag between sales and receipts.]

Item o, "Starting Cash," can be *the* plug figure for a new enterprise, that is the amount of outside capital that must be attracted to keep item q, "Cumulative Cash Flow," positive. Try doing your early projections with zero starting cash in order to determine how deep the "hole" is and when the worst case (the "hole") occurs. By approaching the projections in this way, you and your associates force onto paper the nitty-gritty dynamics of the business—what it takes to pay the bills required to build the company. *If you can't do a cash flow projection with confidence, you don't understand the business you are trying to start.* If you *won't* do a serious cash flow projection that others can critically review, you are kidding yourself about wanting to succeed in big-league entrepreneuring.

From the cash flow projections come the other two major financial indicators you will need: projected operating statements (profit and loss statements) and projected balance sheets. A skeleton operating statement looks like this:

OPERATING STATEMENT

	19XX	19XY	19XZ
Sales			
Cost of Sales			
Gross Margin			
Marketing			
Management			
Engineering			
Administration			
Other			
Operating Profit			
Taxes			
Net Profit			

A skeleton balance sheet looks like this:

BALANCE SHEET

	19XX	19XY	19XZ
Assets			
Cash			
Inventory			
Accounts Receivable			
Buildings, Equipment			
Total Assets			
Liabilities			
Accounts Payable			
Loans			
Net Worth			
Capital Invested			
Earnings Retained			
Total Liabilities & Net Worth			

Of course, on the balance sheet, which is a snapshot of the financial circumstances of the company at a specified point in time, the sum of the assets must add up to the sum of the liabilities plus the net worth.

There are literally dozens of fine, readable textbooks which include information on how to develop financial statements such as the three described briefly above. Therefore the details of doing so have not been included in this "Guide to Preparing a Business Plan." Suffice it to say that one or more people on the founding management team must be at home with the financial and accounting side of the business.

The funds flow and financial projections section of the business plan summarizes all of the previous sections in terms of dollars coming and going. At a minimum, this section will include the following covering a period of typically two to five years from the start of the business:

- Projected cash flow projection
- Projected operating statements
- Projected balance sheets

With this information, reasoned "guesstimates" about the future dollar value of the company can be made. In addition, the magnitude and timing of money needs should be known. Now, questions of the appropriate legal form of the business—partnership, corporation, etc.—as well as the nature of any "deal" with outside investors can be productively addressed.

8.0 OWNERSHIP

Once the requirements of the business to be built are identified via a thoughtful planning process, the question of ownership form and percentages can be tackled. It should be obvious that a highly experienced, two-person founding team of venture in need of $2 million in startup capital faces a somewhat different situation than a young, five-person team in need of only $200,000. That's why general rules for deal making are of limited value. They never fit the particular circumstance. The overriding principle is quite simple, however: All the primary participants should feel that any deal finally made is fair. Smart outside investors don't want to put money into a company with an unhappy management team that feels it got screwed. And smart founder/managers don't want unhappy investors who walk away (or sue) the next time money is required or the first time the company bumps into a crisis.

The relative merits of regular corporations versus Subchapter S corporations versus partnerships versus research and development partnerships will not be covered here. There are a number of sources of advice on the subject. Your best guidance should come from your chosen legal help (see commandment one). Likewise, the merits of common stock versus convertible preferred stock versus various debt instruments are beyond the scope of this guide. What the ownership section of your business plan should show is your conclusions on these matters plus a recommended financing and ownership scheme covering the time period used in the financial projections.

What should the ownership split be in a startup? Consider the simplest case first. Suppose $1 million is needed for a new venture and it has two founders who will personally invest $250,000 each. It's clear that the two founders will keep at least 50 percent of the business. If they have a lot of germane experience and have worked long and hard to develop a plan and line up people, it's also clear that they have strong arguments for retaining more than 50 percent of the company for their $500,000 in cash. It is likely that if their venture excites prospective investors, the entrepreneurs can raise the missing $500,000 they need by *selling* somewhere between 20 and 40 percent of the company (thereby keeping 60 to 80 percent).

Consider a more complex case. Suppose, once again, that $1 million is needed for a new venture. But this time assume there are four prospective founders, two of which have key technical ideas and expertise and two of which have broad relevant business experience. None of the four is able to invest any part of $1 million, but all four will have to leave high paying jobs to join the new enterprise. What's fair in this instance? Chances are that the founding team in total can end up with 10 to 40 percent of the company over time via stock options, staged financing, and other agreed upon mechanisms. This percentage assumes the founders are dealing with professional investors and advisers. It might be possible for the founders to retain a higher percentage if they are willing to "get in bed with" less financially sophisticated investors (the so-called "dentists and doctors circuit"). But this alternative has other drawbacks that must be considered by the founders of a potential high-risk business. For example, later rounds of financing from professional money sources may become quite difficult if the company's ownership is already spread around somewhat indiscriminately. There are a variety of ways to compensate key, noncash contributors to a startup operation. A legal firm with rounded new enterprise experience will have seen many combinations and permutations. You don't need to reinvent the wheel.

What if no outside money is needed at all? Suppose two, three, or more people happen onto an opportunity and they can finance the startup themselves. In this case, any ownership split is pretty much a matter of negotiation between the parties with this proviso. At the earliest possible moment after the business plan is formulated, all the parties involved in the ownership should agree upon and sign a written buy/sell agreement that spells out precisely what procedures will be followed in the event that one or more of the parties wishes or is forced to disengage from the enterprise. The time to hammer out such an agreement with the help of an attorney is before the company gets going. Do it "now." Tomorrow is frequently too late.

The ownership section of a business plan should cover the entrepreneur's program for financing the business over time including:

- The legal form of the enterprise.
- The nature of the initial financing envisioned, including pricing and the resulting ownership distribution.
- The nature of projected future rounds of financing, including planned pricing and the resulting ownership distribution.
- The projected returns that any investors will enjoy on the money they have invested in the enterprise.

This last element of information, the projected returns, can then most handily serve as the centerpiece of an overview that you, the writer(s), may wish to prepare and include at the very front of your business plan.

The fourth commandment stresses the importance of developing a written plan. Such a plan may turn out to be nothing more than an exercise. Done properly, a plan is really a simulation of the proposed undertaking, done in advance, using the best available information and judgment. The blueprint is a representation, not the house itself. The results of the planning effort may be negative ("it won't work"), or the requirements for success (economic viability) may be too high or risky, given the possible returns. More likely than not, the very effort required to sweat through the development of a comprehensive plan will dissuade many potential entrepreneurs, and thereby, possibly save them from the pain of failing. Business building in these times is not a sure thing. "Far better it is to dare mighty things . . . ," said Teddy Roosevelt. Getting the "things" down on paper is a useful filtering process before you dare.

Appendix B contains a table of contents for a business plan based on this "Guide to Preparing a Business Plan."

EXERCISE

Appendix C contains a complete business plan for a new enterprise, the Cdex Corporation. It is an actual plan that was reviewed by a number of active venture capitalists in late 1981 and early 1982. Read the plan yourself and evaluate it. What, in your opinion, are its important strengths and weaknesses? Jot them down on the sheet provided. Then look over the venture capitalists' comments on Cdex that follow in the Epilogue to Appendix C.

5

The Fifth Commandment

Employ key people with proven records of success at doing what needs to be done in a manner consistent with the desired value system of the enterprise.

People do what they like; they like what they know. Experience adds depth to knowledge. The best indicator of how a person will perform in the future is how he or she has done in the past in the same or related activity. Criteria for selecting key people is dictated by the plan, the blueprint, for the business. A brickmason is not needed to construct a wooden building. The plan reflects the operational objectives, the work-a-day culture, and the intentions of the primary participants. The interests and capabilities of a key new person must harmonize with all three.

Commandment one dealt with the primary participants—directors, advisors, officers, and unique employees. Commandment five has to do with setting the stage for the expanding and ultimately much larger group of people upon whom a growth company sooner or later must depend.

There are two sides for the key-people coin. One side has to do with qualifications in a technical or functional sense; the other has to do with what can best be termed attitude, or, in somewhat fancier terms, proclivity to pitch in and enthusiastically extend the particular values of the budding enterprise. The proper selection of exactly the right key people is akin to adding sturdy wall studs to a house under construction. Sound decisions made early on in picking lead salespeople, department supervisors, foremen, senior technicians, and plant superintendents (all examples of "key" people) greatly simplify the addition of wallboard, siding, roof joists, and shingles later.

CASE M. Ralph X's itch to run his own show became unbearable, and he shopped around for an opportunity he could get his arms around. After a number of months he found something that really excited his imagination. He found it literally right in his own backyard. Ralph was an avid small boat sailor, and he was at the time the champion in his class of high performance, two-person boats, a prominent class in the area. One Saturday after racing Ralph found out that the manufacturer of his boat was on the brink of bankruptcy, primarily due to mismanagement by the boat's designer (who was also the boat company's owner and president).

Ralph checked into the matter, analyzed the situation in depth, prepared an extensive business plan, and raised $200,000 from a group of eight individuals during a period when most other entrepreneurs were having difficulty in getting money. Ralph left his middle management job, put together a smart board of directors, hired a sales vice-president with extensive boating industry experience, and prepared to set up boat production. He purchased the fiberglass molds and exclusive rights to the design and name from the then-defunct boat designer and manufacturer. A lot of Ralph's time the first few months was spent assuring dealers across the country that there would be plenty of new, quality boats to sell by the following spring season. He then turned to manufacturing. For a variety of reasons, Ralph hired the original boat designer, call him Y, to head up production. Y picked a plant site on the nearby coast, hired a crew, lined up suppliers, and started building boats for Ralph according to the schedules called for in the business plan.

To cut a long, painful story short, the promise of the business plan was never fulfilled. Y produced poor quality, overly costly boats that were shipped into the distribution/dealer system. Ralph scrambled to identify and correct the problems. It turned out that the plant was in a poor location and the supply of knowledgeable, dependable labor was erratic at best. By the time Ralph replaced Y and relocated the plant, the damage to the boats' reputation in the field was severe and a boat selling season had passed. During the period of troubles, two new competitors with comparable boats entered the picture. Ralph was never able to regain the momentum he had started with, despite his expenditure of a lot of extra money on advertising to the trade. He borrowed the money to finance the extra advertising, and he (unwisely, in desperation) personally signed a guarantee for the loan to his company. Five years later Ralph is still paying off the debt out of the salary he earns working for a large real estate firm.

Hindsight is always 20/20, of course, but it is clear that for entrepreneurs there is no substitute for hiring proven experience in doing what the enterprise needs to be done. In this case, Ralph needed someone who had produced high quality, relatively high priced, fiberglass units in volume within tight cost parameters. What he got was a nice guy who loved the boat and had made several thousand of them essentially one at a time.

Entrepreneurs are always under time pressures, very often self-imposed. Expediency sometimes prevails over tight thinking. Nowhere is it as costly to err as in the selection of people around whom essential functional or technical activities will revolve.

How do you protect yourself? Here are four suggestions:

1. Tough face-to-face discussions
2. Reference checks
3. Scenario questioning
4. Multiple interviewers

1. Tough face-to-face discussions. Entrepreneurs tend to be outgoing and optimistic in nature. It goes with the territory. You like to be liked. Most people do. It's natural to look for the best in people; doing so makes for a smoother world. Most anyone you are going to interview for a key position is going to have at least fairly good oral skills (especially salespeople). You've got to cut through the fuzz and get to the heart of the matter. *What specifically has the person done and accomplished during the last five years?*

Use the interviewee's resume or application as a chronological guide and then ask open questions ("Tell me about . . .") to dig out exactly what the candidate has done every month for the past sixty months. Press for details. Make notes. Clarify discrepancies. Question gaps. Identify accomplishments. When you are done with the interview you should thoroughly understand the candidate's "proven record" and his or her feeling about it. If you are not comfortable extracting such details, turn the job over to another primary participant who is.

2. Reference checks. With sixty months of activity in hand you are well equipped to verify the highlights and gather additional insight into the key person you are considering adding to the team. Phone two or more references and ask them to tell you about the candidate. Seed the conversation with specific questions from your notes in order to refresh memories. In particular, try to pick up extra input on the candidate's attitude (more about this later in this commandment) and personality. You are not necessarily looking for someone who "fits in" in a conforming sense of the word. But in a smaller company the chemistry between individuals is important. There's nowhere to hide. Besides, the more you know about someone, the better you will be able to guide and help him or her succeed in your company.

3. Scenario questioning. In a second or third meeting with a candidate, pose some "what if" questions. For example, think back to Ralph and his fiberglass boat company. Suppose he had asked Y one or more of the following questions:

"Tell me, Y, what specifically would you do if we found that our production costs per boat were running 25 percent over budget two months in a row?"

"Say, Y, how would you respond to a sudden increase in orders—say ten or twenty more boats per week than had been planned?"

"What would you do if a union tried to organize the plant?"

"Tell me about your approach to inventory control, Y."

"Outline for me, if you don't mind, how you would go about assuring that we have zero defects shipped to our customers."

Y's answer to that last question would probably have been a humdinger!

Scenario questioning can help you separate those people

who really know what they're about and those who are playing it by ear and only hoping they can handle whatever arises. It's the difference between bears and cubs, wine and grape juice. It's OK to hire cubs and grape juice as long as you know what you are getting and you are willing to fill in for the lack of relevant experience and seasoning in one way or another to get done what needs to be done, in accordance with your business plan.

4. Multiple interviewers.   No matter how bright you are, Mr. or Ms. Entrepreneur, you will still tend to hire in your own image. For that reason alone it is useful to get other people's reactions to people you are considering for key positions. Beyond that reason, some of your colleagues may be better than you in sniffing out hidden flaws or weaknesses in people upon whom you are going to depend if you are going to progress beyond the sandbox stage and really father or mother a company that is moving toward the big time. One reason commandment one urged the formation of a team with consistent values was so important decisions could be processed through more than one person. Have others interview interesting candidates for key positions. Listen to your associates' opinions and reactions. Synthesize the evaluations. Every hiring decision entails some risk. The worst case is to get someone on board who is so-so. He or she is not good enough to promote and not bad enough to fire. By arranging multiple interviews and using your directors, advisers, other founders, and trusted confidants, you can at least shoot to minimize the risk in the always touchy art of evaluating people.

Assessing the technical or functional side of the key-person coin takes work. Once that work is done, the issue of the second side of the coin, the attitudinal or values side, comes up for thoughtful consideration.

There is a growing body of literature on the phenomenon increasingly known as "corporate culture." A corporate culture is normally hinged to a set of values. The explicit values in a given company's culture may run the gamut from how to dress to how to deal with customer problems and subordinates. A set of implicit values in a given company picks up where the explicit ones leave off. Over time, the combination of stated and unstated rules of behavior (values) permeate a work force, for better or worse. On-the-job behavior gravitates toward certain accepted norms, and newcomers violate the norms at their peril. Every established company has a culture. Not every management team in the galaxy of established companies, however, has the corporate culture it wants.

Experience indicates that it is quite difficult to greatly change a culture once it has a firm foothold. Logic suggests that the ideal approach for an alert growth company management team is to consciously define a desired value pattern early in the life of the organization. From that point on, it is a matter of cultivating the targeted culture via the managers, supervisors, activities, and reward systems of the enterprise.

There is a growing list of major companies who are adopting a rather (but not completely) rigid policy of only hiring people at the entry job level and only promoting from within. "We grow our own," is the underlying thesis. And it is clear that the consistency in values across, say an IBM, a TI, a 3M or an AT&T, is largely a product of such a policy. But a new venture can hardly invest time and money to develop its senior people from scratch. It needs experienced help to execute the dictates of the business plan. So what's to be done?

The conflict between wanting to "grow your own" people and, therefore, your own culture or value system, and needing people "now" who can perform expertly in a technical or functional sense their first day on the job is best resolved in two ways. First, the criteria for hiring must be broadened beyond the usual technical considerations. People with specific *values* must be sought at the same time as you are looking for a salesperson or an accounting supervisor with four years experience. Second, each new employee needs a minimum of eight hours of value orientation during his or her first three months with the company. That's how the conflict can be at least partially resolved. This resolution takes time up front during which the entrepreneurs think through what they themselves are about. This resolution takes time in the field to ferret out qualified people. This resolution takes executive time month after month because only the top people in a rapidly growing company can transmit values so that they "stick to the ribs."

CASE N. Three middle-aged men formed a company dedicated to the proposition that an average product, very superior customer service in very narrow market segments, and a forty-hour week for each of them were compatible with making a lot of money. Within four years the company had grown to over a thousand em-

ployees and gone public at a very attractive price as
well. Over half the employees were involved with customer service in one way or another. Early on the three
partners formulated their "philosophy." Each new employee from about number twenty-five on was (and is)
fed this philosophy almost incessantly. The key elements
in the founders' own words are as follows:

Any and every company problem is your problem.
(Don't pass the buck or point the finger.)
Glitter on your own time. (Don't worry about status
symbols and showing off on the job.)
We price and sell service, not technology or products.
Let the customer take advantage of you.
Finish and put your name on every task you start.
Bake the incentives into the work itself.
Pace company growth to staff growth.
Simplicity rules.
Know your customer's shoe size.

A year ago, two of the three founders retired for positive
reasons to pursue other interests. The company is continuing
its dramatic, almost textbook, growth. Unplanned turnover
in the company is virtually zero.

CASE O. The management of a successful midwestern
company has organized itself so that one of the four top
officers of the company is available for three hours each
Monday morning to sit and talk with all employees hired
during the past week. The meeting is loosely structured.
He or she uses some slides and some flip charts, but
mostly the officer puts himself or herself into the delivery, the value orientation. The management is currently considering expanding the effort so that all the
company's employees have lunch with an officer at least
once a year in small groups of six to ten people.

CASE P. A two-year-old company in Southern California
will only hire salespeople who have recently completed
their college degrees at night or in a co-op (work-study)
program. "We find that people with such backgrounds
are twice as tenacious and productive as other sorts of
people we have tried. They fit in with the way my wife
and I run the business," the president said. "We believe

in twelve hour days with a long vacation once a year to recharge the batteries."

Technical or functional skills are only part of what it takes to build a large company from scratch. A new enterprise must hire people with needed skills in its early days. An entrepreneur misses an important opportunity, however, if he or she doesn't also look for people amenable (judging from past practices or disposition) to having "more than a job." Building a company is a rewarding experience, even fun. There's normally ample satisfaction to go around. But it takes a conscious effort to cultivate and maintain anything better than a neutral culture.

6

The Sixth Commandment

Reward individual performance that exceeds
agreed upon standards.

---

*Performance above the perfunctory level is a discretionary
matter for each employee. Most people have alternative, off-
the-job ways of utilizing excess energy or talent. Channeling
such excess into activity beneficial to the business requires a
tailored approach to each individual. A manager must first
insure that there is an understanding of the minimum results
to be achieved. Then, for performance above the minimums,
forms of compensation important to the performer—or in
some cases, teams of performers—must be utilized.*

Commandment one spoke to the importance of consistency
among the primary participants in a new enterprise. Commandment five suggested action to promulgate a conscious
value orientation throughout an organization as it expands,
recognizing full well that diversity will increase with success
and size. Commandment six calls for a sharp break with the
past in that it admonishes the builders of new companies to
do away with general, all purpose reward systems.

People work for many reasons. This has always been the
case. But "bread winning" is not the common denominator it
once was. Today's work force has an incredible collection of
individuals from all walks of life, each more liberated in one
way or another than he or she would have been even ten
years ago.* It is necessary for management to align the ef-

---

* For a detailed analysis of current trends, see Daniel Yankelovich,
New Rules (New York: Random House, 1981).

forts of individuals and the end results sought by the organization as a whole. It is folly to think that general profit sharing plans or benefits packages or promotion criteria or a quarterly beer blast or arty pictures in the lobby are going to stimulate or reinforce desired behavior across the population of the enterprise. "Forms of compensation *important to the performer*—or in some cases, teams of performers—must be utilized."

Conventional wisdom suggests that every employee wants to get rich, be promoted into positions of larger responsibility, have his or her medical expenses paid for, work in pleasant surroundings, have a nice boss, be "fulfilled," and retire with a substantial nest egg. Much of this thinking by corporate pacesetters is based unknowingly on Abraham Maslow's famous 1940s hierarchy of needs paradigm.

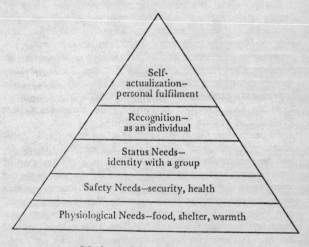

Maslow's Hierarchy of Needs

Maslow postulated that people had an endless series of needs, starting at the bottom with physiological needs, and progressing upwards. As a given need level became satisfied, a new need emerged and "drove" or "motivated" the individual onward and upward—a continual striving all the way to the open-ended top, the ever elusive self-actualization. Maslow's hierarchy has provided the theoretical underpinnings of a great deal of what has gone on under the heading of motivation and personnel work the past forty years. It replaced piecework as the "secret" to what makes employees tick. The question is, does it fit the realities of the 1980s and 1990s? At least one modern researcher, Daniel Yankelovich, thinks not.

Maslowism: The Biggest Trap of All*

The quest for self-fulfillment borrows its forms of expression from whatever sources are most convenient. Unfortunately, the materials closest to hand have been an odd combination of the psychology of affluence, reinforced by an outlook whose interwoven tenets proclaim: live for the moment, regard the self as a sacred object, be more self-assertive, hold nothing back.

Where did those assumptions come from?

Early in the postwar quarter-century, the ideas of "more of everything" and the "primacy of self" merged in a school of thought that may be called "self" psychology. Self psychology received its most influential expression in the work of the psychologists Abraham H. Maslow, Carl Rogers, and Erich Fromm. Their thinking spread throughout the culture, with the help of self-help movements such as est and books with titles such as Looking Out for No. 1, How to Be Your Own Best Friend, *and* Pulling Your Own Strings.

In particular, the theories of Maslow ingeniously combine a psychology of affluence with a vision of inner development. In the 1950s, Maslow posited a hierarchy of human needs that has become part of the conventional wisdom of our time. According to the hierarchy, people who are preoccupied with meeting "lower-order needs" for food, shelter, and economic security have little energy left for pursuing the "higher-order needs" of the spirit. Vital energies are released to the search for "self-actualization" only when the lower-order needs have been met. We move up the hierarchy of needs in an orderly fashion, on an escalator of increasing affluence.

There is obviously some sense in which human priorities do function according to a hierarchy. When we are sick, all that counts is getting well. When our survival, physical or economic, is threatened, it powerfully

---

* From *New Rules—Searching for Self-Fulfillment in a World Turned Upside Down* by Daniel Yankelovich. Copyright © 1981 by Daniel Yankelovich. Reprinted by permission of Random House, Inc.

concentrates the mind (as Samuel Johnson observed about the prospect of being hanged). But the idea that self-actualization—the highest achievement of which human beings are capable, according to Maslow—presupposes our ascension through various stages of economic well-being is a peculiarly self-congratulatory philosophy for a materialistic age.

In Maslowism, the self-actualized person who steps off at the top of the escalator is a particular personality type. He or she is assumed to be a creative, autonomous self, virtually independent of culture. The theme of the creative individual, independent of culture, is to be repeated over and over again in the literature of self psychology and its pop-psychology progeny. One of Wayne Dyer's books speaks glowingly of the theory that "you are the sum total of your choices."

By now, millions of Americans have garnered extensive—and painful—experience in personal struggles with the new, Maslow-inspired duty-to-self ethic. It has, to be sure, some benefits to offer the individual, but the core idea is a moral and social absurdity. It gives moral sanction to desires that do not contribute to society's well-being. It contains no principle for synchronizing the requirements of the society with the goals of the individual. It fails to discriminate between socially valuable desires and socially destructive ones, and often works perversely against the real goals of both individuals and society. It provides no principle other than hedonism for interpreting the meaning of the changes and sacrifices we must make to adapt to new economic-political conditions.

Where does that leave the entrepreneur? Conventional wisdom says everyone wants to strive upwards; the economic and social reality of the current decade suggests that such wisdom is fast becoming obsolete. Here is a sequence of thinking that experience indicates will work in a modern setting. First, you need to establish a personal point of view that says that an important part of your particular job as a founder/manager is to help other people succeed in your organization. You have to appreciate that a critical segment of your time has to be devoted to being a super coach (achieving results through others) rather than being the star player. As your enterprise grows, the percentage of time devoted to "coaching" should gradually increase for most members of the management team. Graphically, the progression looks like this:

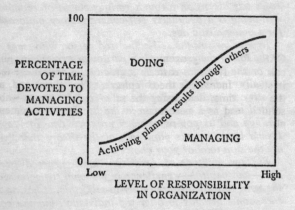

PERCENTAGE OF TIME DEVOTED TO MANAGING ACTIVITIES

DOING

Achieving planned results through others

MANAGING

Low   High

LEVEL OF RESPONSIBILITY IN ORGANIZATION

The inability of entrepreneurs to change their managing style (to "manage" more and "do" less) is one of the most common reasons why many of them no longer fit well with their company as it successfully grows up. More on this in commandment ten. A second step in the sequence is to establish agreed upon standards with those involved. The overwhelming evidence on employee performance that both academics and practitioners have uncovered over the years is that people tend to respond to structured expectations. They need to know—want to know—where the goal lines or boundaries are, what the name of the game is, the shape of the target, how high is up, what are the acceptable minimum results. Lest you think that these phrases are merely clichés, spend some time chatting with a cross section of employees in a lunchroom or two. Ask about their work-a-day concerns; listen carefully to their vocabulary. People in a work-a-day world want to know what is expected of them. As one engineer put it, "I can't hit a home run if no one pitches to me."

The point is that the practice of managing with objectives covered in commandment three has to be percolated down through the organization to the individual employee level.

Corporate objectives become meaningful when they are translated into what it is that a given man or woman is to achieve in, say, the next thirty, sixty, or ninety days.

The third step in the sequence of working with modern employees is to insure that the reward systems of the enterprise support and reinforce the desired behavior *and* are consistent with the interests of the particular individual.

> **CASE Q.** The management of a young specialty chemicals company in the eastern United States was interested in steadily increasing the company's sales volume and, at the same time, decreasing the sales-force expenses—absolutely and as a percentage of sales. The management also espoused decentralized decision making. The president finally settled on a system that a) effectively raised the salespeople's commission on orders obtained, shipped, and collected in their well-defined territories, and b) gave each salesperson precisely $500 a month for expenses, no more and no less. This shifted the operating decisions about travel, entertainment, how to spend time, and whether to stay overnight at the Hilton and eat a steak to the individual in the field. If a salesperson spent less than $500 for expenses in a given month, he or she pocketed the difference (as income). And he or she had to weigh the cost of any sales and sales commissions lost by underspending on travel and entertainment expenses. If a salesperson wanted to spend more than $500, he or she could spend it—out of his or her own pocket.
>
> The company is continuing to grow at a five year compound rate of over 60 percent. Salesforce turnover has been very low.

Not everybody is driven by money. Dual promotion ladders whereby individuals can advance in status and responsibility (and salary) without moving into managing jobs are becoming more common, especially in higher technology companies. In many phases of science and engineering it's almost a full-time job today just to keep current. To compound that burden with the additional tasks of getting results through others invites both frustration and, perhaps, failure. Entrepreneurial innovations in organizational design can be as important as technical breakthroughs.

CASE R. The founder/managers of an exciting new entry in the business-machine field decreed early on that the company would have no "dead-end" jobs. Today the company has sales exceeding $100 million. It has no private secretaries, but it does have a very modern, multipurpose internal communications system. The company has no janitors or guards; it does have subcontractors who provide those services. Each new employee is guaranteed a job change opportunity within two years of his or her starting date as well as three performance appraisals during the interim. No profit center (business planning unit) can exceed 500-700 employees without becoming a candidate for division into two or more profit centers. The company farms out all manufacturing and subassembly work that is expected to become standardized and routine.

Can the management of Case R hold to its "no dead-end job" principle when the company has 5,000 and then 10,000 employees? Certainly it can't without trying!

There is a strong case to be made for the fact that as the population ages, and as mobility slows, working people are increasingly looking to their employers to be more responsive to a broader range of human needs than in the past. This phenomenon presents managers and executives with one of their greatest opportunities. It may also present them with a duty, but for certain there is an opportunity.

The opportunity is to make the modern corporation an integral and imaginative part of the evolving social fabric of the times. Most of the larger, established companies of today were formed and shaped before the 1960s. The burst of entrepreneurial activity in the late 1960s was largely technologically based. The renaissance of entrepreneuring in the 1980s has a much broader raison d'être, one that reflects the passing of the traditional industrialism with its steel mills, assembly lines, and relatively small percentage of college educated adults in the work force.

The new entrepreneurialism is based on a pluralistic society with many discrete, unique markets. It is based on a population of knowledge workers who are rather intent on achieving "personhood" for themselves in an infinite variety of forms. And it is based on the enduring need for human contact and relationships, not in spite of the march toward individual recognition, but in addition to it.

*Now all the evidence of psychiatry . . . shows that
membership in a group sustains a man, enables him to
maintain his equilibrium under the ordinary shocks of
life, and helps him to bring up children who will in turn
be happy and resilient. If his group is shattered around
him, if he leaves a group in which he was a valued
member, and if, above all, he finds no new group to
which he can relate himself, he will under stress, develop
disorders of thought, feeling, and behavior . . . The
cycle is vicious; loss of group membership in one generation may make men less capable of group membership
in the next. The civilization that, by its very process of
growth, shatters small group life will leave men and
women lonely and unhappy.*

George C. Homans, *The Human Group**

Entrepreneuring is more than capitalizing on an opportunity spawned by knowledge and the times. It is a force for
change and human resource development that transcends a
set of products or services and markets that are attractive at
a particular point in history.

---

* William G. Ouchi and Alfred M. Jaeger, "Type Z Organization: A
Corporate Alternative to Village Life." *Stanford Business School
Alumni Bulletin,* Fall 1977–1978, p. 13.

7

The Seventh Commandment

Expand methodically from a profitable base
toward a balanced business.

---

*Optimism is both the poison and the antidote of the growth
company manager. It may be possible to accomplish all
things, but not simultaneously. With limited resources, sequential growth over time is the judicious prescription for
prosperity. Seek logical, incremental extensions of existing activities, but avoid a growth for growth's sake psychology. Bigger is not automatically better; more is not necessarily merrier.
Make managing a competitive advantage. Increase customer
dependency on the enterprise. Economic success can breed
more of the same and/or other returns for the primary participants. Money is the traditional reward; life-style considerations are becoming more widespread.*

You can't build a skyscraper on sand. A balanced business
doesn't just happen. Sometimes you have to bunt to get on
first base. Walk before you run. Avoid growing into trouble.
All of these aphorisms tend to ring true in the cold light of
day. But historically, expanding methodically has proven to
be something of an unnatural act for those who start new
companies . . . and even sometimes for experienced entrepreneurs who try to turn around old ones. In 1981, Roy Ash,
cofounder of Litton Industries and later director of the Office
of Management and Budget in the Nixon administration, was
fired as the chairman and chief executive officer of the
money-losing AM International (formerly called Addresso-
graph-Multigraph). As reported in *Fortune*: ". . . Ash's big

blunder was his failure to build a solid foundation of profits before making acquisitions."

How does an entrepreneur protect himself or herself from the harmful side effects of optimism, the tendency to see an opportunity under every rock? First and foremost, he or she must have a deep sensitivity to the mechanics of profitability—basic profit math.

"We make, or expect to make, 20 percent on sales." "It's going to give us 30 percent before taxes." "Product A will make money every day of the year." These kinds of common statements reflect an important and widespread misconception that many people picked up somewhere along the way, often in grade school (on that day the local merchant stopped by to introduce business to the class). The misconception goes like this: Every dollar of sales has a portion of profit in it. Here's the picture.

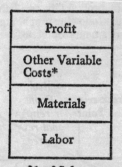

$1 of Sales

* Note: "Variable" costs are those costs that vary with volume, e.g., labor, materials, freight, sales commissions, packaging, etc.

Look familiar? The problem is, of course, that it is wrong. There are *no* pennies of profit in a sales dollar until all the fixed costs of the enterprise are covered. A more useful way to visualize the situation is this.

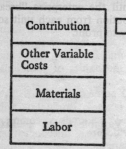

Contribution to:
1) fixed costs, and then
2) profit requirements.

For example, if the fixed costs (management salaries, rent, insurance, etc.) of a new venture are projected to be $100,000 for its first year in business, no profit will be made until that $100,000 is paid.

The mechanics of profitability can handily be summed up and illustrated on the following graph, a graph that at various times goes under the name of break-even chart and profit-volume chart.

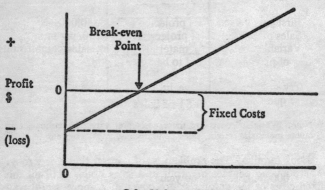

Sales Volume—Units or $

The vertical axis is profit; the horizontal axis is sales volume. At zero sales, the amount of profit is a loss (negative profit!) equal to the fixed cost of the time period under study.

If each unit sold and sales dollar received does indeed have a contribution (defined in more detail below), then the fixed cost is gradually nibbled away until the enterprise "breaks even." After that point, the contribution from each unit sold and sales dollar received goes totally to profit.

Here, briefly, is the idea.

Sales Price — Variable Costs = Contribution per sales $ or unit of sales

Fixed Costs ÷ Contribution = Break-even Point in terms of sales $ or units

Total Sales Income—(Total Variable Costs + Fixed Cost) = Profit

Now, for the purposes of commandment seven, the important issue to recognize is that there are three fundamental elements in the profitability of a company:

Sales Volume . . . in units or dollars
Fixed Costs . . . for the time period
Contribution . . . per unit of sale or dollar of sales

For example, suppose you were working on a new venture with these essential facts.

First year's fixed costs projected to be $550,000.
Sales price of product projected to be $100/per unit.
Variable cost (labor, materials, freight, sales commission) of product projected to be $45 per unit.

Try graphing the above information enroute to answering these questions:

• How many units will have to be sold to break even?
• What will the sales volume in dollars be at the break-even point?
• How much profit will the company make if it sells 25,-000 units during the year?

Do your work on the graph below.

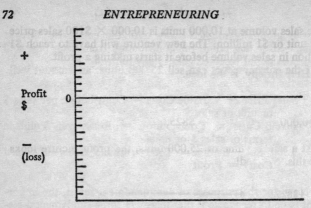

Profit
$

+

0

—
(loss)

Sales Volume—Units or $

The math works out as follows:

Sales Price	$100	
Variable Costs	−45	
Contribution	$55 per unit	
$\dfrac{\text{Fixed Cost}}{\text{Contribution}} = \dfrac{\$550,000}{\$55/\text{unit}} = 10,000$ units to break even.		

Graphically, the above looks like this:

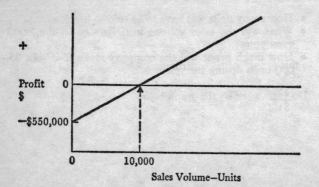

Profit
$

+

0

−$550,000

0   10,000

Sales Volume—Units

The sales volume at 10,000 units is 10,000 × $100 sales price per unit or $1 million. The new venture will have to reach $1 million in sales volume before it starts making a profit.

If the entrepreneurs can sell 25,000 units, an amount well above the break-even point, the profit will be as follows:

$2,500,000 Sales Income—($1,125,000 Variable Costs + $550,000 Fixed Cost) = $825,000.

At a sales volume of 25,000 units, the profit picture looks like this. Not bad!

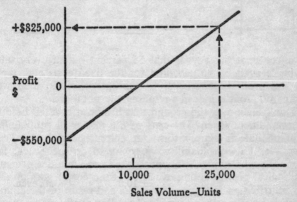

Sales Volume—Units

Now, one more important refinement to understanding these basics. In actual practice, the contribution is usually converted to a percentage, a contribution *rate*.

$$\frac{\text{Contribution per unit}}{\text{Sales Price per unit}} = \text{Contribution Rate.}$$

In this example, the contribution rate was:

$$\frac{\$55}{\$100} = 55\%$$

Graphically the contribution percentage looks like this:

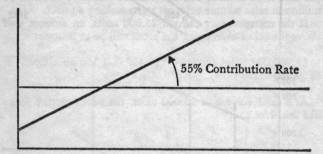

55% Contribution Rate

In effect what this says is that 55 percent out of every sales dollar is available to pay, first for the fixed costs and, then, for the profit *requirements* of the enterprise. In a growth company, profit is indeed a requirement, not a luxury.

Think back over the ground that has been covered here in commandment seven. The crux of the matter of profitability fundamentals is simply this. An entrepreneurial team can harm—or kill—profitability by trying to do too much, too soon. For what typically happens when opportunities overrule methodical growth is that overhead (fixed costs) goes up and the contribution rate goes down. The end result of the diluted effort is greater sales volume and eroding profitability—not a formula for long-term happiness.

Consider the following example of sales and profits for the Widgetronics Company, Inc.

	1980	1981	1982
Sales	$1,000,000	$3,000,000	$10,000,000
Profits	$ 100,000	$ 200,000	$ 0

Upon analysis, the deterioration of Widgetronic's profitability looked like this. (You don't have the figures to do the analysis, but please note the factors driving profitability down.)

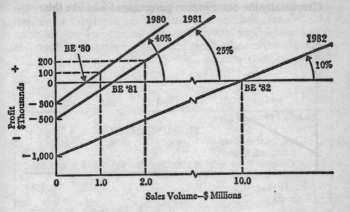

In table form, the analysis looked like this:

	1980	1981	1982
Sales	$1,000,000	$3,000,000	$10,000,000
Profits	$ 100,000	$ 200,000	0
Fixed Costs	$ 300,000	$ 550,000	$ 1,000,000
Variable Costs	$ 600,000	$2,250,000	$ 9,000,000
Contribution Rate	40%	25%	10%
Break-even Point	$ 750,000	$2,200,000	$10,000,000

The company is going downhill quite dramatically.

What did Widgetronics management do between 1980 and 1982? Certainly the team increased sales. ("Look at our 300 percent growth over last year!") But in the process, the fixed costs tripled, and perhaps more importantly, the contribution rate was allowed to drop precipitously from forty cents per sales dollar to ten. By 1982, Widgetronics had to sell $10 million of business *just to break even* at year end. Unless there are compelling strategic reasons to do so and plenty of money to play with, such performance is unacceptable in the turbulent eighties.

An even more detailed analysis of how Widgetronics grew itself into trouble indicated that between 1980 and 1982 it added two major new product lines, one closely related to the base business and one not. Here are the highlights of the impact the additions had on the contribution rate and the fixed costs. Note carefully what the new, unrelated product line brought to Widgetronics.

	1980	1981	1982
Original Product Line			
Sales	$1,000,000	$2,000,000	$ 4,000,000
Contribution Rate	40%	30%	40%
Associated Fixed Costs	$ 300,000	$ 300,000	$ 400,000
New Product Line (Related)			
Sales	0	$ 500,000	$ 2,000,000
Contribution Rate		20%	10%
Associated Fixed Costs		$ 100,000	$ 200,000
New Product Line (Unrelated)			
Sales	0	$ 500,000	$ 4,000,000
Contribution Rate		10%	—20%*
Associated Fixed Costs		$ 150,000	$ 400,000
*Variable costs exceeded selling price			
Totals for Widgetronics			
Sales	$1,000,000	$3,000,000	$10,000,000
Contribution Rate	40%	25%	10%
Fixed Costs	$ 300,000	$ 550,000	$ 1,000,000
Break-even Point	$ 750,000	$2,200,000	$10,000,000
Profits	$ 100,000	$ 200,000	0

In this hypothetical example, a combination of factors hurt the profitability of the company in 1982. New, unrelated product lines are not categorically troublemakers. But they should be approached with caution, and detailed planning.

If you personally are not comfortable working with and manipulating numbers in the way illustrated above, make sure at least one of the primary participants on your entrepreneurial team is!

As in any business, Widgetronics management has but three basic ways to increase the profitability of the enterprise. They can seek to increase sales volume (of products with positive contribution rates), reduce fixed costs, or increase the contribution rate. And there are also three specific ways to increase the contribution rate:

Increase selling prices.
Decrease variable costs.
Change the product mix being sold so as to increase the *net* contribution rate for all products.

Of course, in the Widgetronics example, as in real life, a combination of actions appears to be required.

Profits don't just happen. Like sales, they typically have to be made to happen. Entrepreneurs must have a sensitivity to the dynamics involved. Profitability isn't a luxury, it is a necessity in a growth company. Without it there are no earnings to "retain." Without earnings on today's business it's usually difficult to attract either equity or debt capital to finance tomorrow's. Profitability is the progenitor of cash, and when you are out of cash, you increasingly tend to be out for good in these undulating economic times.

Entrepreneurs are naturally disposed toward spotting opportunities—new product possibilities, additional markets, processes that are twice as good, exciting shortcuts that will mash costs, etc. Their job is to move society from the old to the new. But a fragile new enterprise will be "lucky" if it can do a single thing exceptionally well and consistently during its early years. It may be possible to accomplish all things, but not simultaneously. With limited resources, sequential growth over time is the judicious prescription for prosperity.

8

The Eighth Commandment

Project, monitor, and conserve cash and credit capability.

Cash flow is the blood of a growth business. A company's ability to continue is determined daily, not at year end; by the contents of the checking account rather than the financial statement. Keeping money in hand or readily available for both planned and unplanned events is not only prudent but necessary in unsettled times. Cultivation of financial sources is an enduring duty.

Probably no other commandment has been validated more broadly and visibly since conception than this one. Cash gets consumed in many ways, some of them quite unexpected. In the 1980s, a continuing credit squeeze plus spooky markets for new stock and debt offerings is driving even the largest corporations into wild new patterns of financing themselves. Most of the new patterns involve paying very high interest rates. As chronicled in the *Wall Street Journal*, "Last year [1980] interest expense amounted to nearly 45 percent of corporate net profit before taxes, up from only 14 percent in the 1960s, according to Henry Kaufman, the chief economist at Salomon Brothers." The article goes on to say that, "Getting hooked on short-term debt has made U.S. corporations more vulnerable to recession than at any time since the 1930s." The interest to profit ratio was even worse in 1981.

The squeeze on cash for operations due in large part to interest payments on borrowings is one example of how unplanned events can cripple companies, regardless of size.

A second cash sump that periodically catches high growth

company managements napping is inventory. During the mid-1970s recession, scores of semiconductor companies found themselves with months and months of product on hand, and no customers. The cash accounts on the balance sheet dwindled; the inventory accounts ballooned. But you can't pay the payroll with inventory. More than one emerging company found it necessary to let key people go, a high price to pay for failing to protect cash reserves as the economy slowed. Apparently the lesson was learned by the time the early-1980s recession rolled around, when the semiconductor industry was credited, in general, with keeping its inventories in tune with the times.

The third great cash consumer tends to be accounts receivable, the money your customers owe you. Without intending to do so, many entrepreneurs start out with a manufacturing or services company and end up with a bank (of sorts)!

> **CASE S.** A young, well-degreed couple started a consulting business aimed at cashing in on the booming racquetball, squash, and indoor tennis market. They offered a full range of services based on their own backgrounds and athletic prowess. They could give a client a turnkey package, everything from court layout and building design to retail merchandise selection and club management procedures. The couple did very well during their first two years in business. They even expanded into wholesaling certain types of equipment (special shoes and racquets, clothing for left-handers, etc.). In their third year they got their "big break"—a contract with a major developer to do a chain of twelve racquet complexes in five southwestern cities. The contract required concentrated effort stretching over a fifteen-month period.
>
> The two consultants billed the developer for fees and expenses at the end of each month. When they had not received any payments after the third month, they expressed some concern to their client. He assured them the delay was strictly administrative and that a check was in the mail. A month later they received a check for the first month. But no more checks were forthcoming. By the end of the sixth month the couple had invoices outstanding of over $150,000, and they had incurred over $35,000 in out-of-pocket expenses for lodging,

food, and continuous travel to the client's twelve sites. The client repeatedly assured them the delay was only temporary.

They engaged an attorney. She went after the developer. He fired the two consultants. They went to court. In the meantime, their successful, pre-"big break" business was derailed. To date (eighteen months later) they still haven't collected but a portion of the money they claim they are due. But they still show it on their balance sheet in accounts receivable. Is there a moral to the story? Yes. Don't become a banker unintentionally.

Usually, the management of a new enterprise assumes that it must conform to the prevailing practices of the industry or industries in which the new enterprise will operate. If the industry standard is to allow net thirty days on the payment of invoices, then the entrepreneurs allow net thirty days. Doing so is very understandable. But two questions should be asked. One, if the new company does indeed have a "better mousetrap" of some sort, does it need to meet the industry standard? Two, what actions will be taken if whatever standards are adopted are violated by customers?

Many entrepreneurs shy away from these types of administrative issues. They are hardly the stuff dreams are made of, particularly in the early days of a new venture when everyone is aglow with visions of empires, self-fulfillment, service to society, capital gains, or all of the above. But you are admonished to recognize the cold fact that a business without cash is like a sailboat without wind. Depending upon who's aboard, sitting dead in the water may be interesting, even fun, for awhile. But at some point, survival becomes an issue. Projecting, monitoring, and conserving cash is not an optional feature of entrepreneuring. It is the major part of a high level, heavyweight task for one of the primary participants. The remaining part of that task is the continuing cultivation of financial sources.

The thrust of this book has been toward building growth companies. Almost by definition, growth companies need more money than they can generate internally. That incremental money has to come from outside. The range of normal outside sources is pretty well known:

Individual investors (the "public")
Private investors (wealthy individuals)

Professional investment funds (venture capitalists)
Foundations (money for special causes)
Corporations (joint ventures and equity investments)
Debtors (banks, SBA, individuals)
Credit companies (special forms of debt)
Suppliers (extended payment terms)
Customers (payments in advance)
Employees (stock purchases, wage/salary concessions)

Chances are that sooner or later you will have to rely on one or more of these ten sources to supply some additional wind for your sails. The time to go after money is before you need it!

It is a well-known phenomenon that it's relatively easy to get a loan when you've already got plenty of cash on hand. In that circumstance your credit is five-star (or AAA) and the creditor has no worry about getting repaid. It follows that the time to cultivate relations with potential future sources of capital is when you are doing well, meeting your plan, and running smoothly. Essentially what the entrepreneur must do is inspire confidence on the part of others—confidence in his or her management team, the business concept, and the future of the combination. How is this efficiently done? Pick one or two target sources from the list of ten and court them from day one of the new enterprise.

One of the key products of your business plan, your blueprint, is a thoughtful indication of how much money is required at various points along the way in the early years of the business. The business plan—or more likely, updated versions of it—can be your basic tool in courting potential sources of later rounds of financing. Let your targeted individuals read it. Ask for comments. Then keep the intended investors informed of progress.

In addition, include your targeted sources in periodic mailings. Visit them. Draw them into the life of the company in ways convenient to you. Should you let your potential sources of future debt or equity know why you are cultivating them? Of course! You're not playing a game with your business. You are going after needed funding in the same way you would go after needed raw materials or vital parts or a person you would like very much to hire. There's nothing sacred about money. It just happens to have more mystique than other business ingredients. Go after it. There's generally more money around than there are good, thought-out, business ideas and plans. Once you've done your homework, figure "they" need you more than you need them. This is not to suggest arrogance on your part, merely conviction.

There is evidence of the dawn of a new day for modern business management. The old day featured a rapidly growing population, essentially unlimited natural resources, cheap energy, a stable currency, low interest rates and low inflation, relative isolation from overseas competition, and a compliant work force that understood hard times. The new day features just the opposite. And the hard times of the transition which began in earnest in 1973 are especially aggravating to the most recent generation of employees who had come to take good times, economically speaking, for granted. As the dawn gives way to the new day, managers in general will have to return to the fundamentals.

Productivity is already a battle cry across the nation. The effective use of people at all levels is becoming fashionable, but it will receive increasing attention, particularly at the white collar level. Marketing will be tightened up in many ways. For example, the proliferation of "me-too" products will fade as the buying public increasingly seeks real value, rather than the cosmetic appearance of value. And cash is returning to favor over various forms of debt collected over the years under the guiding star of leverage. Entrepreneurs by nature tend to favor hard cash over paper anyway. The new day of the 1980s is made for them.

9

The Ninth Commandment

Maintain a detached point of view.

Managing a growing business requires unyielding dedication that can consume the body, impair the senses, and warp the mind. Such effects are harmful to the individual and the enterprise. Clinical objectivity is the only preventive. Growth implies and entails risk. Risk begets failure as well as successes. Wide perspective gained through nonbusiness experience or study helps one endure the pressures and accept with equanimity the results, good and bad, of business decisions.

Few new ventures get very far without a lot of what has become known as "sweat equity," the investment of many, many long, long days of toil by the key people. Just why this investment seems to be mandatory is unclear. It may be a law of the universe. It may have something to do with giving birth to a new entity. The explanation may reside with the fact that entrepreneurs typically have sizeable egos, so they try to do everything themselves. Whatever the cause, when there is an excessive amount of such equity invested over time by one or two individuals, the size and health of the total enterprise is going to be constrained.

CASE T. Sam J., aged thirty-six, was hired away from a large electronics firm to be the general manager of a startup company. The company was founded and financed by two older, private investors and a venture capital fund. The company did well and within a year

Sam was made president. During that year fourteen-hour days were the norm for Sam as he hired, fired, sold, billed, designed, cajoled, figured, and, on occasion, worked on the production line. Sam was the hub of the wheel, and as the company grew, he took pride in knowing every employee and every issue.

The company prospered, but by the third year Sam was stretched too thin. His board prevailed on him to add three vice-presidents, who for the most part were not strong people. Probably subconsciously, Sam tended to hire dependent subordinates so that his position as the hub remained undisturbed.

The flourishing company sold stock to the public and moved into its own new factory during its fourth year. That same year Sam and his wife built a new home high on a hill near the factory. The axis of the new home was aligned with the factory, and the living room bay window looked directly down on it. Sam often invited groups of employees other than his officers to dinner. (He invited officers on occasion.) The dinners were one of the many ways Sam was able to keep his finger on the pulse of the operation and perpetuate his network of information sources within the company. Sam continued his twelve-to-fourteen-hour days. Everyone felt he set an excellent example.

The growth of the company slowed in its fifth year. Sam took it quite personally and chided his vice-presidents to work harder. The problems which seemed to be overtaking the company included a lack of new products, a rather primitive accounting and control system, aging production processes, and weak marketing. Sam attacked all of the problems. A downturn in the economy aggravated the situation. At that point Sam became desperate. During one week he fired two vice-presidents, signed a $200,000 contract with a consulting firm to diagnose the company's situation, and triggered a violent oral exchange with the two founders regarding the source of the company's fall from grace in terms of performance.

Within four months the founders had sold their sizeable block of the company to an acquisition-minded conglomerate. The conglomerate picked up the rest of the pieces of the company at a bargain price six months later.

Was Sam a hero or a villain? A very thin line separates the two in the world of entrepreneuring. He gave the enterprise what it needed in the early days. In the process, his personality became inseparable from the business itself, and the vital element of objectivity was lost. People didn't work for the company, they worked for Sam. Sam wasn't the president of a growth venture, the captain of the company's management team. He was a self-appointed king of the realm. The company didn't fail; it outgrew its leadership and then collapsed when the single hub could no longer support the weight of the enlarged wheel.

Sam's inability to step back and put some distance between himself and the enterprise is a common problem. It is particularly visible at the entrepreneurial end of the sequence of stages through which most successful companies pass. Over the last ten years, several scholars have analyzed various companies in an effort to discern any distinct and recurring patterns. Most notable among the studies was a comprehensive one done by Professor Larry E. Greiner of the University of Southern California. Overall, the conclusion reached by the researchers is that, indeed, there are some common stages and crisis points, and that an appreciation of them can assist top managers in piloting their enterprises through time. The most important stages in the corporate metamorphosis are illustrated in the diagram, "Typical Stages of Growth."*

As companies become older (x-axis) and larger (y-axis), they usually also become more complex because of either product line or market expansion, or both. As a given company becomes more complex, the managing practices used by the key people need to change; often the structure of the company has to change as well. Stage one in the diagram, growth through entrepreneurship, is the subject of this book. One person or a small group works long, hard, informally, and quickly to launch a new enterprise. A certain percentage of the startups succeed because of the energy applied, but the single-minded dedication of the early executives often also contains the seeds for the first crisis: the crisis of thin management. The entrepreneur tries to do everything; he or she won't let go of some of the reins, the company's needs exceed the grasp of the one or two individuals in the driver's seat; the enterprise bumps off the road to success.

* Adapted from article by Larry E. Greiner, "Evolution and Revolution as Organizations Grow," *Harvard Business Review*, July–August 1972, p. 41.

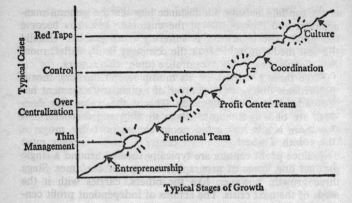

What does it take to stay on the upward growth curve, to continue succeeding beyond what is typically the first crisis point? Usually it takes a broadening of the management talent base, some effective staffing that adds up to the well-rounded functional team needed for stage two growth. Such a team might include accounting or manufacturing or marketing experts depending on the needs of the business and the voids in the entrepreneur's expertise. In this second stage the entrepreneur, if he or she is to make the transition personally, must begin getting results through others, as opposed to through his or her own individual efforts. Many entrepreneurs find this a tough transition to make, and many don't make it. Sam in Case T above illustrates the point.

In companies where the leadership hurdle is cleared, progress up the growth curve often continues, products and markets are typically added, the business prospers and also becomes rapidly more complex. The stage is set for the second major crisis, centralization. The single level of general management normally found in a functional organization gets to the point where it simply can no longer efficiently handle the increasingly diverse issues, problems, and questions flooding in from the various functional vice-presidents. (Refer to section 6.0 in the "Guide to Preparing a Business Plan.") There is a general management overload. Schedules start being missed. Budgets get overrun. Communications bog down. Silly mistakes are made. And the quality of decisions at the top falls because the distance between the general management and the realities at the customer base has become too great. The enterprise is suffering from success. Usually the best medicine is to break the company into smaller, more manageable pieces—to decentralize into profit centers.

Stage three growth, with its multiple-profit centers, means that at least one additional layer of general management has been added to the organization. This suggests that key decisions are once again made closer to the customer base, and that there is a more homogeneous character to the range of issues with which each profit center general manager must deal, since profit centers are typically formed around a single product line, piece of geography, or type of customer. Stage three growth, however, like the others, carries with it the seeds of the next crisis. The actions of independent profit centers breed the crisis of control.

Profit center managers have a tendency to go off in their own directions. The total enterprise, then, becomes merely the sum of the parts, instead of more than the sum. Corporate management gets increasingly uneasy as it senses that it's losing touch with what is going on. The objectives of the enterprise become fuzzy as it stretches in various directions. Overall, things get out of control. Coordination is needed in order to exploit competitive advantages systematically—on a company-wide basis. Such coordination, stage four of growth, usually takes the form of added management information systems, reporting mechanisms, and a more rigorous planning and performance review schedule throughout the year. In short, more meetings, manuals, and memos—the bane of the traditional entrepreneur!

These moves, in time, do bring about a higher degree of coordination. Experience indicates that they also can usher in the next crisis—red tape. The busy business builders in the emerging company find they are spending two-thirds of their time justifying what they do during the remaining third. The control systems developed for the decentralized company become anchors instead of sails. How is the red tape cut, or thinned, without letting the pieces of the enterprise come apart? A variety of human overrides to control systems have been tried. Examples include task forces, matrix structures, and administrative maneuvers to promote the productive interaction of seasoned people for the good of the whole organization. These overrides are sometimes successful, but not particularly enduring. A new slant on how to accomplish optimal coordination in companies with increasingly diverse activities (products/services/markets/technologies) is that the necessary control and value systems need to be *internalized* across the organization in at least the key players. Such internalization suggests the development of a corporate culture, a term introduced in commandment five. The word culture implies that a group of people share a point of view about matters important to a larger enterprise of which they are a part. For more on how to accomplish this, see *The Art of Japanese Management*, referenced earlier in commandment four. You may also want to see *Theory Z* by Bill Ouchi.*

The important point to recognize overall is that the management actions that breed success at one stage (like "sweat equity" invested during the entrepreneurship stage) carry with them the seeds for the next crisis. *It is necessary for entrepreneurs to change their managing style as the company prospers.* What worked yesterday is not the formula for tomorrow. A sensitivity to this issue of managing style is requisite to achieving a degree of the clinical objectivity called for here in the ninth commandment.

What else is required? Good health, including adequate rest, and some semblance of a balance between vocational and avocational interests probably fills out the picture sufficiently for this book.

Few people appreciate the physical wear and tear required to found and run a dynamic enterprise. Any busy manager or executive can tally the litany of meetings, phone calls, airports, rent-a-cars, airplanes, hotel rooms, deadlines, and more meetings and say "whew." Now add to this litany the incremental need you have when you are entrepreneuring to initiate everything, the absence of staff support, and the overhanging potential personal cost of being wrong or ineffective at any given point in the day, and you essentially double the load on the individual, the entrepreneur, the person who's his or her own boss.

The only antidote is physical and mental fitness equal to the load. Self-help books by the hundreds prescribe appropriate routines for getting and/or staying in shape. And any competent M.D., especially one associated with preventive medicine (the entrepreneurial end of medicine), can help you tailor-make a program compatible, within reason, with your

* William Ouchi, *Theory Z—How American Business Can Meet the Japanese Challenge* (Reading, Mass.: Addison–Wesley, 1981).

own life-style. Likewise, regarding mental health, particularly stress, there is a growing body of knowledge about what causes stress and how to deal with it. A foremost authority in the matter of stress is the late Dr. Hans Selye, M.D., emeritus professor at the University of Montreal and president of the International Institute of Stress.

Dr. Selye, among others, pointed out that at its roots, stress is the body trying to readjust or adapt itself to a new situation. The situation can be good or bad, real or imagined. This is a very important point to appreciate. Your body actually reacts to each of the following kinds of events.

A threat by a mugger on a city street.
Receipt of a huge order for your company.
A death in the family.
Leaving on a vacation trip to Europe.
A sudden shortage of cash to pay bills.
The apparent failure of a key subordinate to meet expectations.

Each good, bad, real, or imagined event (the "mugger" may just be a shadow) causes a physical reaction of one sort or another, whether it be an increased pulse and breathing rate triggered by adrenaline or a feeling of malaise brought on by hormones or ". . . newly discovered brain substances, endorphins and enkephalins; and activities of the nervous pathways that mediate and alter the stress response."*

Dr. Selye put the situation this way. "They (the events) produce a body change—in effect, a derangement. And, having done so, they also make a demand on the body to readjust itself. This demand is nonspecific. It requires adaptation to a problem regardless of what the problem may be.

"That is to say that all agents [heat, cold, running, drugs, hormones] to which we are exposed produce not only their specific actions but also a nonspecific increase in the need to perform certain adaptive functions and then to reestablish normalcy—and the nonspecific is independent of the specific activity that caused the rise in requirements. This nonspecific demand for activity as such is the essence of stress.

"It doesn't matter whether the agent or situation we face is pleasant or unpleasant. All that counts—from the standpoint

---

* Hans Selye, "On Executive Stress," *Executive Health*, October, 1981, p. 2.

of stress-producing, or stressor, activity—is the intensity of the demand for readjustment or adaptation.

"If it seems difficult to see how such different things as heat, cold, drugs, sorrow, and joy can provoke an identical biochemical reaction, nevertheless it can be demonstrated by actual quantitative biochemical measurements that certain reactions of the body are totally nonspecific and common to all types of exposure.

"Stress is not something to be avoided; in fact, it cannot be avoided. As the response to a stressor, a stimulus, a set of circumstances that induces a change in the flow of physiological and/or psychological functioning, it's inevitable and as essential and useful a part of living as changes in breathing and blood circulation produced when exercise is the stressor.

"Depending upon their intensity and the way they affect the individual, stress reactions can be pleasurable as well as helpful. *But when they are inappropriate or excessive, they can exhaust the capacity to respond and lead to difficulty—emotional distress, behavioral disturbances, or symptoms of illness.*"*

Dr. Selye went on to say that included on the list of stress-related diseases are peptic ulcers, high blood pressure, and many others.

Now what does all this mean to the entrepreneur? It means that whether the fledgling business does well or poorly, the absolute number of significant events (good and bad, real and imagined) cascading down on the founders and managers is likely to be high. When the number of events is compounded by the indigenous risk of failure in both an economic and a psychological sense, it is easy to understand why stress "goes with the territory," particularly in the earlier stages of growth.

Physical and mental robustness is achieved, like most everything else in life, through conscious effort. The components of such an effort seem to boil down to this list.

- Exercise and food and drink in amounts that result in a physical condition which has a high degree of resilience.
- Purposefulness of one's *chosen* work.
- Avocational interests that regularly require undivided attention.
- Perspective on the risks and rewards of decision making

* *Ibid.*, p. 2.

which is a major component of your professional life-style.
● Simplicity, even in the face of gargantuan success.

Detailed consideration of these components is beyond the scope of this book. But research indicates that the more the matter of physical and mental health in executives is studied, the more these five tend to stand out as signposts along the road to a full life. Since stress itself is a biochemical phenomenon, you need to keep your body well tuned, resilient. Purposefulness is the flip (and positive) side of uselessness and its byproduct, frustration. A serious avocation is like a haircut. You enjoy or at least endure a short respite and come away different—at least temporarily. Decisions are the tracks that change runs on but you can't cover much distance without meeting some ups, downs, and twists along the way. Planning helps you select the optimum routing. And simplicity, from cars and clothes to food and entertainment, is one of the few active defenses against the turbulence of the times.

A wise person once said, "A man is rich who has enough." Enough for the effective entrepreneur is more than just a shot at millionairedom. There are more passive ways to accumulate a large net worth. Entrepreneuring is really a life-style choice, but it has its dangers. A new enterprise, being small, fragile, and even beguiling, can be loved to death, especially by its parents. Excessive affection and the intertwining of personalities with the sinews of the business may be acceptable practices for the permanently small businesses of the world, but they have limited application to high growth, business-building situations.

Does the above point of view preclude wide-eyed enthusiasm and the do-or-die attitudes generally attributed to newly rich entrepreneurs and always espoused by them in speeches *after* they have emerged into the limelight? Of course not. The best analogy is that of a World Series pitcher or a Superbowl quarterback and an entrepreneur. While the contest is on there is no limit to what the leader will pour into the pursuit of victory. And he will exhort his teammates to excel at almost any cost. But when the game is over, the losing pitcher or quarterback doesn't shoot himself or drink himself into a stupor. He accepts what happened, tries to learn from it, goes on living, and aims to win next time. That's professionalism; that's a growing part of entrepreneuring in these increasingly complex times.

10

The Tenth Commandment

Anticipate incessant change by periodically testing adopted business plans for their consistency with the realities of the world marketplace.

The past will not come again. Neither isolation nor insulation from tomorrow is possible. The problems of the times are the opportunities of the times, as always, but the strings attached are multiplying. Governments and new competitors, domestic and foreign, will increasingly affect the conduct of a given business. So will social evolution. Despair is of little value. Vigilance is.

There's no room for entrepreneuring in a static society. So commandment ten carries good news. We are in the midst of a lot of change; the year 2000 is closer to us than 1960; the world has shrunk; and today is the first day of the rest of your life. The clichés abound. But the average person is swept along by events, turning his or her head from side to side occasionally as birthdays flash by. Then the day arrives when the energy required to deviate from the worn path exceeds that remaining in the reservoir, and what might have been will never be. Commandment ten is an admonishment: Take advantage of the turbulence to build something new. Commandment ten is a warning: Systematically keep what you are building finely tuned to the times.

Graphically, the challenges of the times can be depicted this way.

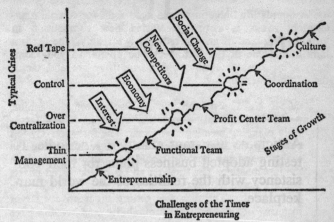

Challenges of the Times in Entrepreneuring

Entrepreneur/managers of growth companies must contend with two kinds of pressures, those from within and those from without. From within, both increasing size and complexity generate various problems and crises. From without, as depicted by the arrows, an increasing number of pressures are exerted on a growing company as it becomes more and more visible. The overriding question for the movers and shakers of a dynamic enterprise is quite simply: What do we do to keep on succeeding? The name of the game keeps changing! There are six specific "what-to-dos" inherent in the dictates of the tenth commandment.

- Recognize and deal with reality.
- Adjust your managing style to fit the changing needs of the enterprise.
- Treat organizational structure as a variable.
- Nurture a process of managing within the company.
- Verbalize information and expectations.
- Remain doggedly customer centered.

These are the actions required to anticipate incessant change in order to amend your plans for the business accordingly.

Recognize and deal with reality. Politics is a reality. Women in the work force at all levels of responsibility are a reality. A population bulge in people aged right for middle management ranks is a reality. Varied new competition in virtually any kind of growth industry is a reality. The list is a long one. Some of the factors can be pivotal to your company. You must determine which ones they are and factor them into your thinking.

> **CASE U.** Throughout the 1970s one of the major, worldwide accounting and auditing firms had a large-scale planning meeting every year. The forty to sixty top people in the firm attended. Early in each meeting the senior managing partner would recount progress since the last meeting. The lines on all his multicolored charts swept gracefully upwards and to the right as the decade moved along. The firm was getting progressively larger in terms of total billings; profitability was keeping pace with billings; and per partner income stair-stepped up quite nicely, year to year. There was some concern that the number of clients in the client base was shrinking slightly over time, but little urgency was attached to the matter in light of all the good news.

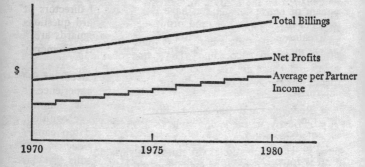

In 1980, the senior managing partner of the firm and his two key associates took a look at the past decade of the firm in constant dollars, that is, with figures adjusted for inflation. Had the trio been a little younger, the findings would have "blown their minds." As it was, they experienced a profound sense of shock. Instead of growing, the firm had actually been shrinking over the last ten years. In real terms, the charts looked like this:

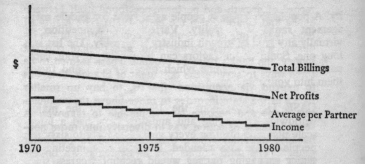

When the drop in total fees, profits, and per partner income was added to the shrinking client base, it was clear that the firm, in total, had "stopped succeeding." The reality was that the firm was starting to fail.

Most competent management teams can respond to reality if they know what it is, but it's easy to see and hear only what's comfortable in the rush of day-to-day events. And subordinates, as a rule, shy away from being harbingers of potentially noxious tidings. One of the most practical safeguards a team of entrepreneurs can have is a board of directors or advisors that is qualified and prone to inject hard questions and realness into the enterprise. Two other safeguards are a proper managing process and regular contact with customers.

Adjust your managing style to fit the changing needs of the enterprise. Any entrepreneur with industrial experience is familiar with the pluses of the "-ions" in a business: communication, instruction, delegation, motivation, and recognition. These -ions don't just happen. Someone at the top causes them to happen, usually both by example and by decree. The ideal is for these -ion elements of "achieving results through others" to be an acquired taste bred into the new company by the entrepreneurs from the start so there is an ever-growing core of talent available to respond to the times. The alternative to breeding is often a crash program of management development triggered by some impending emergency.

CASE V. The management of a relatively young, medium-size bank holding company with an excellent record of growth and performance found itself between Scylla and Charybdis in the early 1980s. The reality of banking was one of deregulation, consolidation in the industry, massive new competition, and tidelike costs of money, the bank's primary product. There seemed to be three ways to survive the onslaught of change. One was to expand via acquisition, that is, to buy up smaller banks in the state in order to move above the medium-size range and become less vulnerable to takeover. A second course of action was to diversify into more nonbanking activities where there appeared to be firmer ground. The third course was to tighten down on expenses and drive short-term performance upward as a prelude to selling the entire holding company to one of several suitors who had made overtures in recent months.

The third alternative was thought by the management to be the least desirable. Upon analysis, however, it was the only viable one simply because the company did not have available the necessary talent and systems required to manage either a lot more banks or nonbanking activities. "The well is near dry," is the way the CEO put the situation. There was sadness in his voice.

Any individual's managing style is composed of numerous components, and it is clear that not every one of them has to be adjusted continuously. For entrepreneurs, the biggest single challenge is usually to let go of responsibility *and* authority as the venture ripens into an ongoing business. Delegating is the operational word. Delegating is not a skill as much as it is an attitude. When you push responsibility outwards and downwards, you do give up something . . . particularly some chances to star. But you and the enterprise also gain eyes, ears, arms, legs, and ideas that will grow stronger and sharper with encouragement and time. A growth business is a team effort—more analogous to professional football or basketball than to golf. Effective teams have good coaches or player/coaches who can change roles with alacrity.

Treat organization structure as a variable. The typical progression in most companies is to move over time from a functional organization structure to a profit center structure, as suggested in commandment nine.

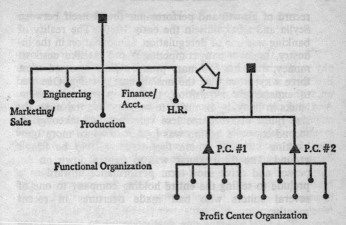

Marketing/Sales

Engineering

Production

Finance/Acct.

H.R.

Functional Organization

P.C. #1   P.C. #2

Profit Center Organization

Such a general progression tends to make sense as it breaks the enterprise up into smaller pieces, develops more general managers, etc. The important point to recognize is that there are countless variations and permutations along the way having to do with position titles, reporting relationships, salary brackets, and all the administrative paraphernalia that goes with keeping a group of humans working together. Ideally, the culture of the company since inception will include a high valuation on flexibility, cooperation, and appropriate competitiveness. At a minimum, entrepreneurs will do well to downplay from the start the significance of the classic status symbols of corporate life that can make for premature hardening of the arteries, that is, structural rigidity in the face of internal and external change.

CASE W. From day one, the four cofounders of a biomed company decided that they would share the decisions and power in the company. This philosophy has permeated the organization which today employs more than 100 people, many of them skilled technologists and scientists. Ramifications of the philosophy include a total absence of private offices and private secretaries, no titles on business cards, group reviews of peer performance, rotating committee chairpersonships, and only a few broad job classifications for salary administration purposes. To date, after fifteen months, the company has met or exceeded all its projections.

Whether the management of Case W can make its philosophy work when it has 500 employees is still an open question. But there is evidence that so far little energy is being burned up with internecine struggles for attention and recognition. And the company is proving to be very adaptable to the changing (and evolving) mix of customer and distribution-system requirements being placed on it. This is an extreme case, but structure in its broadest sense is truly a variable during the company's formative period.

Nurture a process of managing within the company. The key word is *process*. It implies a continuing, consistent, if not repetitive, sequence of events over time during which the participants can get to know one another, come to share a common vocabulary, and establish a sense of order in the life of the enterprise. There are enough surprises in the day-to-day existence of a young company. Irregularities and spontaneousness in the way managers conduct themselves are superfluous, if not downright destructive.

> **CASE X.** A high-flying electronic game company went bankrupt after the heart of its programming and engineering staff walked out and set up shop down the street. Among the deficiencies articulated by the departees were the following:
>
> > Ad hoc salary adjustments (increases) . . . usually only when a person threatened to leave.
> > No information on company plans (and doubts as to whether any plans actually existed).
> > No feedback on either company or personal performance.
> > Lack of confidence in the competence of two of the three top executives. ("They didn't seem to know what they were doing.")
> > Continuous "fire drills" in terms of who was to do what, by when ("Perpetual panic").

In sum, the management function (as contrasted to the programming and engineering functions) of the company was bush league in comparison to the very large market opportunity which the company originally had. What started out as a venture turned into an adventure rather than a business. The original entrepreneurs lost out.

Where does a process come from? As a practical matter, the written business plan can usefully serve as the centerpiece around which a managing process is formulated. An updated business plan is needed for each coming year. Picture a management team that meets a half day monthly solely to review progress and think ahead. Here are the kinds of subjects that could form the skeleton of an annual process.

January	Review actual results against previous year's plan. Agree on strong and weak points. Identify business planning process changes needed.
February	Review performance of key individuals in company. Consider all compensation matters.
March	Identify major market trends and discuss implications. Analyze relations with key customers.
April	Agree upon an economic forecast for the coming twelve months and its probable impact on operations. Crystallize any required action. Write down assumptions.
May	Establish a planning timetable and methodology for the coming year's business plan. Consider what's new in planning techniques.
June	Discuss trends in technology that can affect any phase of the business. Assign "watchers" or resource people to keep current on specific items of interest.
July	Review six month results against annual plan. Note any weaknesses in assumptions. Make necessary revisions for second half.
August	Set corporate and planning unit objectives for coming year.
September	Listen to and discuss plans proposed by planning unit leaders. (Planning unit leaders may be profit-center managers, functional vice-presidents, product managers, etc.)
October	Same as September. Consolidate plans.
November	Review financial and human resource implications and requirements of the consolidated

plan for the company. Present plan to board for comments.

December   Adopt business plan (including budgets) for coming year.

This list of subjects is not meant to be exhaustive, but representative. And a management team that develops *and sticks to* such a calendar tailored to its own enterprise will have gone a long way toward establishing a process that can bring stability, insight, internal consistency, and smarter decisions to the challenges of the times. Of course the above calendar does not preclude the other meetings—planned and ad hoc— that will out of necessity go on. In fact, such a senior calendar can make the interim meetings on more operational matters more efficient because the tendency to jumble short and longer range issues together might well be somewhat diminished.

Verbalize information and expectations. Everybody is in favor of better communicating, but what does it mean? Open offices or an open door policy? Company newsletters? Friday night beer parties for the staff? Casual, mixed level lunches? A formal mentor system? These are all candidates for inclusion, but the heart of communicating is that which has to do with transmitting and sharing ideas, opinions, and critiques on the work being done—the lifeline of the company. The rest, from newsletters to parties, is just icing on the cake for the company on the move. In the final analysis, productive communicating boils down to regular boss-subordinate interchanges about the tasks at hand and those upcoming. And the value of the interchange is amplified if both parties have at least a rough understanding of what the company is all about.

Participation is an overused word with many connotations. But actual day-to-day participation in mainstream events is one of the attractions smaller companies offer to people. Yet it is usually hard to retain that hands-on flavor as a company grows up. It is hard to retain it because the distance expands between the decision makers (customers, founders, officers) and the average employee. It is also hard to retain it because a lot of "nonjobs" get created and perpetuated. This latter problem is starting to get some attention in the 1980s under the general heading of "resizing" (to improve white collar productivity). But the former problem, distance, lingers on. There is no real solution to it other than a chain of managing (from managing managers to managing employees) that is alive and aggressive in helping people succeed in their vocations.

What is it that makes an active chain a necessity? The simple answer is that people do indeed respond to structured expectations. And no matter how this fact is smothered in analysis, a person's boss is his or her primary reference point in the world of work. If that primary point is weak or vacillating, the signal gets through. If that point of reference is ignorant of and noncommunicative on the corporate objectives —where "we" fit in, what's buffeting the company these days, and so on—how is the average employee to be adaptive, enthusiastic, and supportive?

CASE Y. AH&B, a consulting firm, grew rapidly in billings to over $6 million per year. The three founders were able to attract a lot of new talent into the company and, thereby, release their own time for marketing work—the pursuit of new contracts. A giant opportunity in Saudi Arabia captured their imagination—the opportunity to design a complete new city from scratch. The three became enraptured with the project and poured many man-months and dollars into the preparation of an extensive proposal. They flew back and forth to the Mideast, waltzed the Saudi diplomats in Washington, and generally ignored the rest of the activities in their firm. They were oblivious to the resentment that slowly built up among many of the newer recruits who had been charmed aboard personally by one or more of the founders.

The proposal was duly submitted in Saudi Arabia with appropriate fanfare. The date for a decision on the successful bidder came and went. Everybody waited. Then they waited some more. Months passed. The momentum of the firm slowed as first one and then other talented people left—often taking clients with them in the process. The AH&B founders woke up one morning to find they had lost the Saudi bid, they had a shell of a firm in terms of talent still aboard, and their two largest clients of long standing had switched . . . to former employees of AH&B.

Good people don't need to stay on in the dark, and entrepreneuring can be contagious.

Remain doggedly customer-centered. Amid all the external pressures, the ones most important to be responsive to are those that have an impact on your customer base. More than one group of entrepreneurs have been surprised to find that interest rates or foreign competition or a new technological development has suddenly put a big dent in their growth plans. Often the surprise would have been avoided if one or more of the top people had not pushed customer contact, eyeball to eyeball, down low on the list of things to do. For example, a year after the Saudi Arabia debacle in Case Y above, AH&B management received another blow. High interest rates drove AH&B's remaining largest client, a highly leveraged, second home developer, into bankruptcy. The demise could have been foreseen to an alert observer of the times, which someone at AH&B should have been.

How does a new venture get and stay customer oriented? The signals have to come firmly and regularly from the top. The burden is on the entrepreneur.

Commandment ten calls on the entrepreneur to keep on entrepreneuring in the sense of monitoring and responding accurately to the times. Doing so is a key ingredient in "keeping on succeeding," in fanning the flicker of a concept into a roaring flame of success that serves society in some useful way. Given the flame, the challenge shifts to perpetuating it. In 1980, *Business Week* published a study of thirty-seven Fortune 500 companies whose managements are generally considered to have been effective in extending the youthful spirit of their enterprises over many, many years, through good times and bad.* The study indicated that the managements of these companies shared eight common attributes:

- A bias toward action
- Simple form and lean staff
- Continued contact with customers
- Productivity improvement via people
- Operational autonomy to encourage entrepreneurship
- Stress on one key business value

* Thomas J. Peters, "Putting Excellence into Management," *Business Week*, July 21, 1980, pp. 196–205.

- Emphasis on doing what they know best
- Simultaneous loose tight controls

These attributes have their roots in entrepreneuring, and they highlight the concept underlying this book—entrepreneuring is, indeed, the Olympics of capitalism.

Introduction to the Appendices

After completing an effective, practical book, an inspired reader is often faced with the dilemma, "Now that I know all that, what do I do first?" This very natural question is particularly tough to answer for a would-be entrepreneur because he or she is potentially faced with some monumental tasks if dreams are going to be converted to reality. Do you, entrepreneurial reader, at this moment have a business concept? Is there a market opportunity upon which your concept can feed and flourish? Have you identified the precise kinds of people and how much money you will need to translate the concept into concrete? Have you moved your thinking and findings out of your head and onto paper in a reasonably orderly fashion to see if it can withstand hard scrutiny by knowledgeable folks whose opinions you respect? These are the big league questions generally required to systematically get a new growth company properly launched.

Three appendices follow to help existing and would-be entrepreneurs bridge the gap between the Ten Commandments and managing their own going concerns.

Appendix A is a short guide to analyzing an industry or market. It was developed originally by Michael Porter of the Harvard Business School for use there by students in various courses, including courses having to do with small business development. Nailing down the magnitude of the market opportunity in quantitative terms is a chore many entrepreneurs would happily forego. It's much easier to deal with "soft" facts; every entrepreneur "knows" the market is out there. Why bother researching it? And once in a while a shot in the dark does pay off. Once in a while. Appendix A is included as a supplement to both commandments two and four to help you double your probability to twice in a while.

Appendix B provides a simple table of contents for a business plan. The important thing for an entrepreneur to do is to cover the bases, i.e., make sure that he or she has adequately thought about the subjects listed. Substance is more important than form, but don't underestimate the importance of how a finished business plan looks if you are submitting it to professional investors for evaluation.

Appendix C is an actual business plan. Over the years your author has been dealing with new venture plans. He has had many requests for a sample plan. Appendix C is one such plan. The Cdex Corporation plan is not included as a model, but rather as a somewhat abbreviated sample. It has both strengths and weaknesses, promise and problems. You are encouraged to read it critically and to jot down your reactions. Then answer this question for yourself: Did the management team of Cdex significantly increase their chances for business success by getting their thinking down on paper and exposing it to outside review enroute to starting Cdex for real?

Appendix A

How to Conduct an Industry Analysis

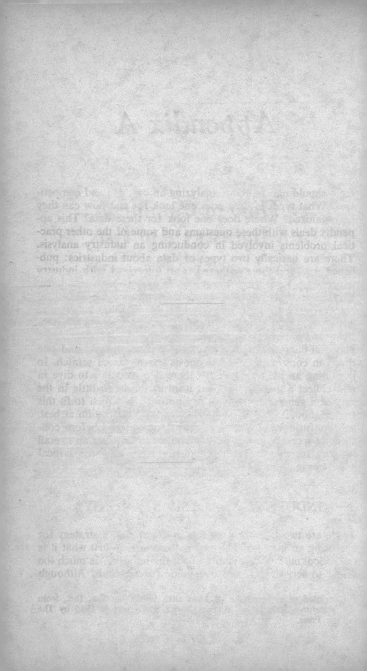

How should one go about analyzing an industry and competitors? What types of data does one look for and how can they be organized? Where does one look for these data? This appendix deals with these questions and some of the other practical problems involved in conducting an industry analysis. There are basically two types of data about industries: published data and those gathered from interviews with industry participants and observers (field data). The bulk of discussion in this appendix will center on identifying the important sources of published and field data, their strengths and weaknesses, and strategies for approaching them most effectively and in the right sequence.

A full-blown industry analysis is a massive task, and one that can consume months if one is starting from scratch. In beginning an industry analysis there is a tendency to dive in and collect a mass of detailed information, with little in the way of a general framework or approach in which to fit this information. This lack of method leads to frustration at best, and confusion and wasted effort at worst. Thus before considering specific sources, it is important to consider an overall strategy for conducting the industry study and the critical first steps in initiating it.

INDUSTRY ANALYSIS STRATEGY*

There are two important aspects in developing a strategy for analyzing an industry. The first is to determine just what it is one is looking for. "Anything about the industry" is much too broad to serve as an effective guide for research. Although

* Reprinted with permission of Macmillan Publishing Co., Inc., from *Competitive Strategy* by Michael Porter. Copyright © 1980 by The Free Press.

the full list of specific issues that need to be addressed in an industry analysis depends on the particular industry under study, it is possible to generalize about what important information and raw data the researcher should look for. Key structural features, important forces causing them to change, and strategic information on competitors are basic areas of inquiry. These are factors that are the target of an industry analysis. However, since these characteristics of structure and competitors are generally not raw data but rather the result of *analysis* of raw data, researchers may also find it useful to have a framework for systematically collecting raw data. A simple but exhaustive set of areas under which to collect raw data is given in Figure A-1.

FIGURE A-1.
Raw Data Categories for Industry Analysis

Data Categories

Product lines
Buyers and their behavior
Complementary products
Substitute products
Growth
    Rate
    Pattern (seasonal, cyclical)
    Determinants
Technology of production and distribution
    Cost structure
    Economies of scale
    Value added
    Logistics
    Labor
Marketing and Selling
    Market segmentation
    Marketing practices
Suppliers
Distribution channels (if indirect)
Innovation
    Types
    Sources
    Rate
    Economies of scale
Competitors—strategy, goals, strengths and weaknesses, assumptions
Social, political, legal environment
Macroeconomic environment

Compilation

By company
By year
By functional area

The researcher who can fully describe each of these areas should be in a position to develop a comprehensive picture of industry structure and competitors' profiles.

With a framework for assembling data, the second major strategy question is how sequentially to develop data in each area. There are a number of alternatives, ranging from taking one item at a time to proceeding randomly. However, there are important benefits in getting a general *overview* of the industry first, and only then focusing on the specifics. Experience has shown that a broad understanding can help the researcher more effectively spot important items of data when studying sources and organize data more effectively as they are collected.

A number of steps can be useful in obtaining this overview:

1. *Who is in the industry.* It is wise to develop a rough list of industry participants right away, especially the leading firms. A list of key competitors is helpful for quickly finding other articles and company documents (some of the sources discussed later will aid in this process). An entering wedge for many of these sources is the industry's *Standard Industrial Classification* (SIC) code, which can be determined from the Census Bureau's *Standard Industrial Classification Manual.* The SIC system classifies industries on a variety of levels of breadth, with two-digit industries overly broad for most purposes, five-digit industries often too narrow, and four-digit industries usually about right.

2. *Industry studies.* If one is lucky, there may be a relatively comprehensive industry study available or a number of broadly-based articles. Reading these can be a quick way of developing an overview. (Sources of industry studies are discussed later.)

3. *Annual reports.* If there are any publicly held firms in the industry, annual reports should be consulted early. A single annual report may contain only modest amounts of disclosure. However, a quick review of the annual reports for a number of major companies over a ten or fifteen-year period is an excellent way to begin to understand the industry. Most aspects of the business will be discussed at one time or another. The most enlightening part of an annual report for an overview is often the president's letter. The researcher should look for the rationales given for both good and bad financial results; these should expose some of the critical success factors in the industry. It also is important to note what the company seems to be proud of in its annual report, what it seems to be worried about, and what key changes have been

made. It is also possible to gain some insights into how companies are organized, the flow of production, and numerous other factors from reading between the lines in a series of annual reports from the same company.

The researcher will generally want to come back to annual reports and other company documents later in the study. The initial early reading will fail to uncover many nuances that become apparent once the knowledge of the industry and the competitor is more complete.

Get into the field early. If there is any common problem in getting industry analyses underway, it is that researchers tend to spend too much time looking for published sources and using the library before they begin to tap field sources. As will be discussed later, published sources have a variety of limitations: timeliness, level of aggregation, depth, and so on. Although it is important to gain some basic understanding of the industry to maximize the value of field interviews, the researcher should not exhaust all published sources *before* getting into the field. On the contrary, clinical and library research should proceed simultaneously. They tend to feed on each other, especially if the researcher is aggressive in asking every field source to suggest published material about the industry. Field sources tend to be more efficient because they get to the issues, without the wasted time of reading useless documents. Interviews also sometimes help the researcher identify the issues. This help may come, to some extent, at the expense of objectivity.

Get over the hump. Experience shows that the morale of researchers in an industry study often goes through a U-shaped cycle as the study proceeds. An initial period of euphoria gives way to confusion and even panic as the complexity of the industry becomes apparent and mounds of information accumulate. Sometime later in the study, it all begins to come together. This pattern appears to be so common as to serve as a useful thing for researchers to remember.

PUBLISHED SOURCES FOR ANALYSIS OF INDUSTRY AND COMPETITORS

The amount of published information available varies widely by industry. The larger the industry, the older it is, and the slower the rate of technological change, the better the available published information tends to be. Unfortunately for the researcher, many interesting industries do not meet these criteria, and there may be little published information available. However, it is *always* possible to gain some important information about an industry from published sources, and these sources should be aggressively pursued. Generally, the problem the researcher will face in using published data for analyzing an economically meaningful industry is that they are *too broad,* or too aggregated, to fit the industry. If a researcher starts searching for data with this reality in mind, the usefulness of broad data will be better recognized and the tendency to give up too easily will be avoided.

Two important principles can greatly facilitate the development of references to published materials. First, every published source should be combed tenaciously for references to other sources, both other published sources and sources for field interviews. Often articles will cite individuals (industry executives, security analysts, and so on) who usually do not appear by accident; they tend to be either well-informed or particularly vocal industry observers, and they make excellent leads.

The second principle is to keep a thorough bibliography of everything that is uncovered. Although it is painful at the time, taking down the full citation of the source not only saves time in compiling the bibliography at the end of the study but also guards against wasteful duplication of efforts by members of research teams and the agony of not being able to remember where some critical piece of information came from. Summary notes on sources or Xerox copies of useful ones are also useful. They minimize the need for rereading and can facilitate communication within a research team.

Although the types of published sources are potentially numerous, they can be divided into a number of general categories, which are discussed briefly below.[1]

Industry studies. Studies that provide a general overview of some industries come in two general varieties. First are

---

[1] L. Daniels (1976) is an excellent general source of business information. There are also a number of computerized abstract services for references and articles available at major business libraries, which can speed the task of finding articles and sorting the useful ones from those that are not so useful.

book-length studies of the industry, often (but not exclusively) written by economists. These can usually best be found in library card catalogs and by cross-checking references given in other sources. Participants in or observers of an industry will almost always know of such industry studies when they exist, and they should be questioned about them as the study proceeds.

The second broad category is the typically shorter, more focused studies conducted by securities or consulting firms, such as Frost and Sullivan, Arthur D. Little, Stanford Research Institute, and all the Wall Street research houses. Sometimes specialized consulting firms collect data on particular industries, such as SMART, Inc., in the ski industry and IDC in the computer industry. Often access to these studies involves a fee. Unfortunately, although there are a number of published directories of market research studies, there is no one place where they are all compiled, and the best way to learn about them is through industry observers or participants.

Trade associations. Many industries have trade associations, which serve as clearing houses for industry data and sometimes publish detailed industry statistics.[2] Trade associations differ greatly in their willingness to give data to researchers. Usually, however, an introduction from a member of the association is helpful in gaining the cooperation of staff in sending data.

Whether or not the association is a source of data, members of the staff are extremely useful in alerting the researcher to any published information about the industry that exists, identifying the key participants and discussing their general impressions of how the industry functions, its key factors for company success, and important industry trends. Once contact with a trade association staff member has been made, this person can in turn be a useful source of referrals to industry participants and can identify participants who represent a range of viewpoints.

Trade magazines. Most industries have one or more trade magazines which cover industry events on a regular (sometimes even daily) basis. A small industry may be covered as part of a broader-based trade publication. Trade journals in

[2] There are a number of published directories of trade associations.

customer, distributor, or supplier industries are often useful sources as well.

Reading through trade magazines over a long period of time is an extremely useful way to understand the competitive dynamics and important changes in an industry, as well as to diagnose its norms and attitudes.

Business press. A wide variety of business publications cover companies and industries on an intermittent basis. To obtain references, there are a number of standard bibliographies, including the *Business Periodicals Index, The Wall Street Journal Index,* and the *F&S Index,* United States (and companions for Europe and International).

Company directories and statistical data. There are a variety of directories of both public and private U.S. firms, some of which give a limited amount of data. Many directories list firms by SIC code, and thus they provide a way to build a complete list of industry participants. Comprehensive directories include *Thomas Register of American Manufacturers,* the Dun and Bradstreet *Million Dollar Directory* and *Middle Market Directory, Standard and Poor's Register of Corporations, Directors and Executives,* and the various *Moody's* publications. Another broad list of companies classified by industry is the Newsfront *30,000 Leading U.S. Corporations,* which gives some limited financial information as well. In addition to these general directories, other potential sources of broad company lists are financial magazines *(Fortune, Forbes)* and buyers guides.

Dun and Bradstreet compiles credit reports on all companies of significant size, whether they be public or private. These reports are not available to any library and provided only to subscribing companies who pay a high fixed cost for the service plus a small fee for individual reports. Dun and Bradstreet reports are valuable as sources about private companies, but since data provided by the companies are not audited, it must be used with caution; many users have reported errors in the information.

There are also many statistical sources of such data as advertising spending and stock market performance.

Company documents. Most companies publish a variety of documents about themselves, particularly if they are publicly traded. In addition to annual reports, SEC form 10'K's, proxy statements, prospectuses, and other government filings can be useful. Also useful are speeches or testimony by firm executives, press releases, product literature, manuals, published company histories, transcripts of annual meetings, want ads, patents, and even advertising.

Major government sources. The Internal Revenue Service provides in the *IRS Corporation Source Book of Statistics of Income* extensive annual financial information on industries (by size of organizations within the industry) based on corporate tax returns. A less detailed, printed version of the data is in the IRS's *Statistics of Income*. The main drawback of this source is that the financial data for an entire company are allocated to that company's principle industry, thereby introducing biases in industries in which many participants are highly diversified. However, the IRS data are available annually back to the 1940s, and it is the only source that gives financial data covering all firms in the industry.

Another source of government statistics is the Bureau of the Census. The most frequently used volumes are *Census of Manufacturers, Census of Retail Trade,* and *Census of the Mineral Industries,* which are available quite far back in time. As with the IRS data, the census does not refer to specific companies but rather breaks down statistics by SIC code. Census material also has considerable regional data for industries. Unlike IRS data, census data are based on aggregates of data from establishments within corporations, such as plant sites and warehouses, rather than corporations as a whole. Therefore, the data are not biased by company diversification. One feature of the *Census of Manufacturers* that can be particularly useful is the special report, *Concentration Ratios in Manufacturing Industry.* This section gives the percentages of industry sales of the largest four, eight, twenty, and fifty firms in the industry for each SIC four-digit manufacturing industry in the economy. Another useful government source for price level changes in industries is the Bureau of Labor Statistics, *Wholesale Price Index.*

Leads on further government information can be obtained through the various indexes of government publications, as well as by contacting the U.S. Department of Commerce and the libraries of other government agencies. Other government sources include regulatory agency filings, congressional hearings, and patent office statistics.

Other sources. Some other potentially fruitful published sources include the following:

- antitrust records;
- local newspapers in which a competitor's facilities or headquarters are located;
- local tax records.

GATHERING FIELD DATA
FOR INDUSTRY ANALYSIS

In gathering field data it is important to have a framework for identifying possible sources, determining what their attitude toward cooperation with the research is likely to be, and developing an approach to them. Figure A-2 gives a schematic diagram of the most important sources of field data, which are participants in the industry itself, firms and individuals in adjacent businesses to the industry (suppliers, distributors, customers), service organizations that have contact with the industry (including trade associations), and industry observers (including the financial community, regulators, etc.). Each of these sources has somewhat differing characteristics, which are useful to identify explicitly.

Characteristics of field sources. Industry competitors will perhaps be the most uncertain about cooperating with researchers, because the data they release have a real potential of causing them economic harm. Approaching sources in the industry requires the greatest degree of care (some guidelines will be discussed later). Sometimes they will not cooperate at all.

The next most sensitive sources are service organizations, such as consultants, auditors, bankers, and trade association personnel, who operate under a tradition of confidentiality about individual clients, though usually not about general industry background information. Most of the other sources are not threatened directly by industry research, and in fact they often perceive it as a help. The most perceptive outside observers of the industry are often suppliers' or customers' executives who have taken an active interest in the whole range of industry participants over a long period of time. Retailers and wholesalers are often excellent sources as well.

The researcher should attempt to speak with individuals in

FIGURE A-2.
Sources of Field Data for Industry Analysis

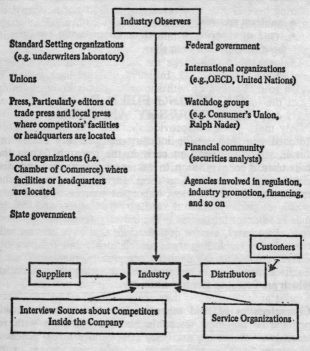

Market research staff

Sales force

Service organizations

Former employees of competitors,
observers, or service organizations

Engineering staff

Purchasing department - in contact
with suppliers who call on competitors

R&D department - generally follows technical
developments and scientific conferences
and publications

Trade associations

Investment banks

Consultants

Auditors

Commercial banks

Advertising agencies

all of the major groups since each of them can supply important data and provide useful cross-checks. Because of their differing perspectives, the researcher should *not* be surprised if they make conflicting and even directly contradictory statements. One of the arts of interviewing is cross-checking and verifying data from different sources.

The researcher can make the initial field contact at any point shown in Figure A-2. Initially, to gather background, it is best to make contact with someone who is knowledgeable about the industry *but who does not have a competitive or direct economic stake in it.* Such interested third parties are usually more open and provide the best way of gaining an unbiased overview of the industry and the key actors involved, which is important early in the research. When the researcher is in a position to ask more perceptive and discriminating questions, direct industry participants can be tackled. However, to maximize the chances of success in any interview, it is important to have a personal introduction, no matter how indirect. This consideration may dictate the choice of where to begin. Field research always involves an element of opportunism, and following a method of analysis should not deter the researcher from pursuing good leads.

It is important to remember that many participants in an industry or observers of it know each other personally. Industries are not faceless; they are composed of people. Thus one source will lead to another if the researcher is adept at his task. Particularly receptive subjects for field interviews are often individuals who have been quoted in articles. Another good method to develop interviews is to attend industry conventions to meet people informally and generate contacts.

Field interviews. Effective field interviewing is a time-consuming and subtle process, but one that will amass the bulk of critical information for many industry studies. Although each interviewer will have his or her own style, a few simple points may be useful.

Contacts. It is generally most productive to make contacts with potential sources by telephone, rather than by letter, or by a telephone call following up a letter. People are apt to put a letter aside and avoid a decision about whether to cooperate. A telephone call forces the issue, and people are more likely to cooperate with an articulate and well-informed verbal request than they are with a letter.

Lead Time. Researchers should begin to arrange interviews

as early as possible, since lead times may be long and travel schedules difficult to coordinate; it may take months to arrange and complete them. Although at least a week is necessary lead time for most interviews, often the researcher can get an interview on very short notice as people's schedules change. It is desirable to have identified a number of alternative sources for any interview trip; if time becomes available they just might be willing to meet on short notice.

Quid Pro Quo. When arranging an interview, one should have something to offer the interviewee in return for his or her time. This can range from an offer to discuss (selectively of course) some of the researcher's observations based on the study, to thoughtful feedback on the interviewees' comments, to summaries of results or extracts of the study itself when feasible.

Affiliation. An interviewer must be prepared to give his or her affiliation and make some statement about the identity or (at least) the nature of his or her client if the study is being conducted for another organization. There is a moral obligation to alert an interviewee if information may be used to his or her detriment. If the identity of the interviewer's firm or client cannot be disclosed, some general statement must be made regarding the economic stake of the firm or client in the business being studied. Otherwise interviewees generally will not (and should not) grant an interview. Failure to disclose the identity of the firm or client will often limit (though not necessarily destroy) the usefulness of the interview.

Perseverance. No matter how skillful the interviewer, scheduling interviews is invariably a frustrating process; many times an interview is declined or the interviewee is openly unenthusiastic about it. This is in the nature of the problem and must not deter the interviewer. Often an interviewee is much more enthusiastic once a meeting has commenced and the relationship between interviewer and interviewee has become more personal.

Credibility. Interviewers greatly build credibility in arranging interviews and conducting them by having some knowledge of the business. This knowledge should be displayed early both in initial contacts and in interviews themselves. It makes the interview more interesting and potentially useful for the subject.

Teamwork. Interviewing is a tiring job and should ideally be done in teams of two if resources permit. While one member asks a question, the other can be taking notes and thinking up the next round of questions. It also allows one interviewer to maintain eye contact while the other takes notes. Teamwork also allows for a debriefing session immediately after the interview or at the end of the day, which is extremely useful in reviewing and clarifying notes, checking for consistent impressions, analyzing the interview, and synthesizing findings. Often much creative work in industry research is done in such sessions. A solo interviewer should leave time for such activity as well.

Questions. Gathering accurate data depends on asking unbiased questions, which do not prejudge or limit the answer nor expose the interviewer's own leanings. The interviewer must also be sensitive not to signal with his or her behavior, tone of voice, or expression what the "desired" answer is. Most people like to be cooperative and agreeable, and such signaling may bias the answer.

Notes. In addition to taking notes, the researcher can benefit from writing down observations about the interview itself. What publications does the individual use? What books are on the shelves? How are the offices decorated? Are they plush or sparse? Does the interviewee have any sample products in the office? This type of information often provides useful clues in interpreting the verbal data that result from the interview and also provides leads for additional sources.

Relationships. It is important to recognize that the subject is human, has never met the researcher before, has his or her own set of personal characteristics, and may be quite uncertain about what to say or not say. The style and vocabulary of the subject, his or her posture and attitude, body language, and so on give important clues and should be diagnosed quickly. A good interviewer is usually adept at quickly building a relationship with the subject. Making an effort to adapt to the style of the interviewee, to lower the level of uncertainty, and to make the interaction personal rather than keeping it on an abstract business level will pay off in the quality and candor of the information received.

Formal Versus Informal. Much interesting information often comes after the formal interview is over. For example, if the researcher can get a plant tour, the interviewee may become much more open as the setting becomes removed from the more formal setting of the office. The researcher should attempt to engineer interviews so that the inherent formality of the situation is overcome. This may be done by meeting on neutral ground, getting a tour, having lunch, or discovering and discussing other topics of common interest besides the industry in question.

Sensitive Data. It will generally be most productive to start an interview with nonthreatening general questions rather than asking for specific numbers or other potentially sensitive data. In situations in which concern over sensitive data may be likely, it is usually best to state explicitly at the beginning of an interview that the researcher is not asking for proprietary data but rather impressions about the industry. Often individuals will be willing to provide data in the form of ranges, "ball park" figures, or "round numbers" that can be extremely useful to the interviewer. Questions should be structured as follows: "Is the number of salespersons you have closer to 100 or 500?"

Pursuing Leads. A researcher should always devote some time in interviews to asking questions such as the following: Whom else should we speak to? What publications should we be familiar with? Are there any conventions going on that might be useful to attend? (A large number of industries have conventions taking place in January and February.) Are there any books that might be enlightening? The way to maximize the use of interviews is to gain further leads from each one. If an interviewee is willing to provide a personal reference to another individual, the offer should always be taken. It will greatly facilitate the arrangement of further interviews.

Phone Interviews. Phone interviews can be quite productive relatively late in a study when questions can be highly focused. Phone interviews work best with suppliers, customers, distributors, and other third-party sources.

Exhibit 1
Index to Standard and Poor's Industry Surveys

Dates of Latest Surveys

IN VOLUME 1	Current Analysis	Basic Analysis
A Aerospace	6-24-76	10-30-75
Air Transport	*6-10-76	4-15-76
Apparel (incl. Footwear)	3-11-76	6-24-76
Autos-Auto Parts	4-29-76	8-12-76
B Banking (incl. Finance & Personal Loans)	8-12-76	7-8-76
Beverages	7-8-76	*......
Building	5-27-76	*8-28-75

		Current Analysis	Basic Analysis
C	Chemicals	5-13-76	12-4-75
	Communication	7-1-76	10-9-75
	Containers	*2-26-76	6-17-76
E	Electronics–Electrical	5-20-76	*9-4-75
F	Food Processing	7-15-76	4-29-76
	Food Processing (Canners, Meats and Dairy Products, and Packaged Foods)	†Discard	†Discard
	Food Processing (Bakery Products, Milling, and Sugar)	†Discard	†Discard
H	Health Care, Drugs, and Cosmetics	3-18-76	7-29-76
	Home Furnishings	4-22-76	2-19-76
I	Insurance	*5-6-76	2-26-76
	Investment	*4-8-76	11-6-75
L	Leisure-Time	8-19-76	11-20-75
	Liquor	§Discard	10-16-75

IN VOLUME 2

		Current Analysis	Basic Analysis
M	Machinery (incl. Rail Equip.)	8-12-76	5-27-76
	Metals Nonferrous	*7-29-76	11-13-75
O	Office Equipment	*4-29-76	8-19-76
	Oil	8-26-76	6-10-76
	Oil–Gas Drilling & Services	5-27-76	....
P	Paper	7-15-76	*8-21-75
R	Railroads	8-19-76	6-3-76
	Retailing (Department, Mail Order, Variety, and Drug Chains)	3-25-76	8-5-76
	Retailing-Food (Supermarkets, Restaurants, and Food Service)	*6-17-76	12-18-75
	Rubber Fabricating	8-29-76	10-2-75
S	Soft Drinks–Candy	§Discard	12-11-75
	Steel–Coal	6-10-76	*9-25-75
T	Telephone	6-3-76	*8-14-75
	Textiles	8-5-76	5-20-76
	Tobacco	7-22-76	5-6-76
	Trucking	*5-6-76	3-25-76
U	Utilities–Electric	5-13-76	7-22-76
	Utilities–Gas	*5-20-76	3-18-76

*Tentatively scheduled for publication during September 1976.
†Supplanted by new, combined Food Processing. §Supplanted by new, combined Beverages. For Candy, see Food Processing.

Subject Guide
VOLUME 1 CONTAINS PAGES A THROUGH L
VOLUME 2 CONTAINS PAGES M THROUGH U

Exhibit 2
Smith Barney Research Service Index

Vol.1   Aerospace
         Airlines
         Automotive
         Building
         Business Services
         Chemicals & Textiles
         Conglomerates

Vol.2   Cosmetics & Toiletries
         Data Processing
         Drugs & Medical Industries
         Electrical Equipment
         Electronics
         Electronics—Consumer

Vol.3   Financial—Banks
         Financial—Insurance
         Financial—All Other
         Food, Beverage & Tobacco
         Food Service & Lodging

Vol.4   Graphics & Office Equipment
         International
         Machinery
         Metals
         Oils
         Paper & Containers
         Personal Care

Vol.5   Publishing & Broadcasting
         Rails, Trucking & Shipping
         Retail Trade
         Rubber
         Utilities
         Miscellaneous

           IR—Industry Review
           TRC—Topical Research Comment
           CR—Company Report
           CFR—Company Financial Report

Exhibit 3
Index to the Value Line Investment Survey

ANALYSES OF INDUSTRIES IN ALPHABETICAL ORDER WITH PAGE NUMBER

Numeral in parentheses after the industry is rank for probable performance (next 12 months).

PAGE

Aerospace/Diversified (8) 101
Agricultural Equip. (9) ..819
Air Transport (11) 251
Aluminum (60) 1153
*Apparel (53) 1601
Auto & Truck (32) 127
Auto Parts-OEM (4) ...826
Auto Parts-Replace (20) 136
Bank (78) 1901
Bank-Midwest (69) 683
Brewing (18) 329
Broadcasting (3) 513
Building (38) 851
Cement (50) 911
Chemical-Basic (40) 551
Chemical-Specialty (30) 1243
Coal & Uranium (26) ..1849
Conglomerates (10) ...1388
Copper (73) 1153
Distilling (70) 338
Drug-Ethical (62) 598
Drug-Health Care/ Hospital Supplies (48) 2012
Drug-Proprietary (79) .1211
Drug Store (16) 792
Dual Fund (12) 1993
Electrical Equipment (13) 1001
Electric Utility-Central (83) 701
Electric Utility-East (75) 1142, 207
*Electric Utility-West (80) 1698
Electronics (43) 1051
Fastener (84) 983
Fast Food Service (29) .1836
Fertilizer (86) 2033
Finance (44) 2001
Food Processing (64) ..1451
Gold Mining (82) 1154

PAGE

Grocery (54) 1533
Household Products (27) 1523
Industrial Services (37) .349
Insurance-Life (6) 1123
Insurance-Divers (42) 239, 1859
Investment Company (41) 1959
Lead, Zinc, Minor Mtls (55) 583
Leasing (1) 202
Machinery (7) 1301
Machinery-Construction & Mining (59) 223
Machine Tool (25) 1370
Maritime (33) 296
Meat Packing (56) 378
Metal Fabricating (39) ..271
Metals & M'ng-Gen'l (74) 1151
Mobile Home (31) 1578
Natural Gas (61) 457
Office Equipment (24) .1082
Oilfield Services (14) ..1350
Packaging & Cont. (28) .954
Paper & Forest Prod. (51) 927
Personal Service (15) ..1813
Petroleum (52) 401
Precision Instrument (35) 170
Publishing & Adv. (23) .1778
Railroad Equipment (45) 287
Railroad-East (49) 642
Railroad-West (21) 1183
Real Estate (63) 661
Real Estate Investment Trust (76) 673, 1232, 1983
Recreation (46) 1751
(Etc.)

*Reviewed in this week's edition.

Exhibit 4
Index to Predicasts Forecasts
Publication Date—July 27, 1976

Note: Updated Predicasts are published on a regular basis.

Appendix B

Table of Contents for a
Business Plan Based on the
Guide to Preparing a
Business Plan Included in
Commandment Four

Guide to Preparing a Business Plan

TABLE OF CONTENTS

4.4 Quality control, packaging, transportation, etc. requirements

4.5 Program for initial time period

4.6 Schedule—who is to do what, by when (Exhibit)

4.7 Budget (Exhibit)

4.8 Results expected (Exhibit)

4.9 Contingency plans

Section 5.0 Marketing

5.1 Method(s) of selling and advertising to be employed

5.2 Product or service features and benefits to be emphasized

5.3 Program for initial time period

5.4 Schedule—who is to do what, by when (Exhibit)

5.5 Budget (Exhibit)

5.6 Results expected (Exhibit)

5.7 Contingency plans

Section 6.0 Organization & People

6.1 Who is accountable to whom, for what. Structure (Exhibit)

6.2 Staffing program for initial time period

6.3 Schedule (Exhibit)

6.4 Budget (Exhibit)

6.5 Results expected (e.g., brief position descriptions)

6.6 Contingency plans

Section 7.0 Funds Flow & Financial Projections

7.1 Projected cash flows from operations; i.e., total funds in and out for the initial time period (Exhibit)

7.2 Proforma profit and loss statements (Exhibit)

7.3 Proforma balance sheets

7.4 Program for monitoring and controlling funds with people and systems included in the Organization planning

Section 8.0 Ownership

8.1 Summary of funding requirements

8.2 Form of business—partnership, corporation, etc.

8.3 Program for raising equity and/or debt money
    required, if any
8.4 Projected returns to investors

Note: If technology is an important ingredient in the
success of the enterprise, a separate section, Technology,
should probably be included in the Business Plan. Such a section would include details on staffing and methods of inquiry
and testing as well as schedules, budgets, results expected,
and contingency plans. A section on technology would normally be inserted after Section 5.0, Marketing.

Appendix C

Cdex Corporation Business Plan
January 1982

The accompanying projections reflect Cdex Corporation management's best current estimate of future operating results. All the figures shown are based upon currently available information and certain management assumptions. Because these projections depend in part upon future events, some of which may be beyond management's control, no assurance can be given that the projections will be achieved.

The following is an actual business plan that was submitted by the management of Cdex Corporation to ten different, practicing venture capitalists in an attempt to raise the $500,-000 needed to carry out the plan. The plan included here is essentially complete. Only a few financial details that were in the actual plan have been omitted. In addition, personal and company names have been changed in some cases to protect the parties involved.

You are urged to read the plan carefully. Assume or pretend you are a potential investor or key employee. What is your evaluation of the plan? Does it seem to be consistent with the ten commandments—particularly number four which includes the "Guide to Preparing a Business Plan"? What weaknesses and strengths strike you as you read the plan? What questions would you ask the Cdex management in a face-to-face interview? Would you be inclined to invest, given sound answers from the management?

Make note of your comments and reactions on the next page as you read the plan. Then compare your thoughts to those of the ten venture capitalists who actually reviewed the plan "for real." Their comments are shown in the Epilogue to Appendix C.

Notes

AN EVALUATION OF THE CDEX CORPORATION BUSINESS PLAN

SECTION	STRENGTHS	WEAKNESSES	QUESTIONS/ COMMENTS
1.0 Concept			
2.0 Objectives			
3.0 Market Analysis			
4.0 Production			
5.0 Marketing			
6.0 Organization & People			
7.0 Funds Flow & Financial Projections			
8.0 Ownership			

Cdex Corporation
Business Plan
January 1982

EXECUTIVE SUMMARY

Over the next twenty years, technology in the form of microcomputers is expected by the founders and management of Cdex to revolutionize the process of training and developing corporate employees. Currently microcomputers are being purchased by businesses and professional people for use on accounting-type applications. Cdex management expects the market for nonaccounting applications of the microcomputer to grow rapidly in the years ahead. Further, Cdex expects to be a leader in providing nonaccounting-type programs. In short, Cdex is aiming to be the first electronic publisher of human resources development materials.

During 1981 four pilot programs were developed, produced, and demonstrated to a variety of potential buyers. In addition, marketing and staffing matters were thrashed out and resolved. The business plan that follows reflects the 1981 work. Management now wishes to raise $500,000 from private investors to take advantage of the opportunity explained in the plan.

I. CONCEPT

Cdex will become the premier electronic publisher of materials for selected market segments in the United States and abroad. Electronic publishing best describes what our company will do; management development material on disks that run on personal computers best describes the nature of our product during our early years. Record publishers sell music on plastic sheets and tapes to which customers listen after inserting the medium into the appropriate machine; book publishers sell information and entertainment on printed and bound pieces of paper which individual customers read at their own pace; Cdex will sell information and performance improvement on floppy disks which corporations and individuals will buy and use in conjunction with personal computers. People taking Cdex programs will personally become more effective and more efficient in their work. Cdex will become an important force in improving "white collar" productivity.

In time, Cdex will have a large library of programs written by a cross section of recognized experts on a variety of subjects vital to the chosen market segments. In the early years, we will concentrate on accepted management development subjects for which there are already proven commercial markets including supervisory training, profit planning, selling skills, managing by objectives, and problem solving. A complete list of the initial forty programs currently under development is included in Exhibit 1, the maiden Cdex information brochure.

The Cdex management team and board feel—based on experience—that there are five major ingredients required if Cdex is to capitalize dramatically on the opportunity being spawned by the well-documented microcomputer boom.

1. Proven subjects (titles) to sell
2. Material in a superior format and medium—superior from the individual users' points of view
3. Dependable delivery systems (microcomputers)
4. Smart marketing, particularly with regards to distribution
5. Sufficient financing to achieve a critical mass of material and market recognition relatively quickly

When present, these five will propel Cdex into the forefront of the embryonic field of electronic publishing.

1. Proven subjects to sell. Two proofs are required for each subject selected for the Cdex library. First, there must be known commercial interest in the subject in the primary segment, the business and professional marketplace. A known commercial interest means that the subject is already commonly taught/bought for management/salesmanship development uses. It may currently be bought in a book, videotape, seminar, manual, or in-house trainer format, but it must already be a popular, purchased development subject. Cdex is not interested in selling both the need for the subject and the medium, only the medium—i.e., computer-assisted, interactive, audiovisual human resource development programs "off the shelf."

The second proof required for admittance to the Cdex library is that the subject have a creditable authority/author behind it. Cdex is a publisher, not (strictly speaking) a creator of materials. We wish to take the best information already available and important to our primary segment and apply modern technology to it to enhance its digestibility, on-the-job use, and benefit-to-cost ratio. The initial programs in the Cdex library were prepared by the author of a best-selling business book, and plans are underway (see later) to expand the stable of Cdex authors starting later this year.

2. Material in a superior format and medium. Interactive, multimedia, self-pacing instruction has long been identified as a powerful *learning technology* in terms of impact, retention, and speed for teaching most (not all) adult/business subjects. This technology has been around for years, but the hardware (delivery systems) and necessary software have not. Now the hardware (microcomputers) is readily available; but a software vacuum already exists and it will mushroom in the years ahead. Cdex will puncture that vacuum and aid the revolution away from manuals, meetings (seminars), and memos . . . where they are not the best solution to the manager and people development opportunity.

Statistics commonly used to illustrate one aspect of the superiority of the technology used by Cdex are those having to do with learner retention of material taught. In general, research indicates that people tend to remember roughly

10 percent of what they hear
20 percent of what they see
30 percent of what they see and hear
60 percent of what they see, hear, and do (interact with)

Cdex programs take full advantage of these findings plus provide individuals with the opportunity to self pace and repeat trips through the subjects. Further, corporate users gain the key advantage of achieving *consistency* over time and across their organizations when Cdex programs form the core of the management development effort. Cdex programs are not subject to the variations in quality and content found in materials delivered live by trainers. For example, technology now makes it possible for all of a company's supervisors to get precisely the same message and retain it.

3. Dependable delivery systems. Microcomputers have come of age very rapidly. Unlike the highly fragmented, single purpose "teaching machine" boom (and bust) of the 1960s, microcomputers are catching on (40 percent growth rate per year) with business and professional people based on solid, varied applications with tangible payoffs. Much of the emphasis at this time is on financial/accounting/number crunching programs ("software"). Cdex management believes there is a substantial opportunity for nonnumber, nongame programs already, and that the company can be a leader in this part of the program market as it expands.

All of the major microcomputer manufacturers (Apple, Radio Shack, TI, Atari, IBM, HP) have extensive machine service networks supporting their multimillion dollar marketing programs. In the 1960s, hardware was a liability for training and development applications. In the 1980s, it is definitely an asset.

4. Smart marketing, particularly with regards to distribution. Given one, two, and three above, Cdex management's marketing concept is to tackle the corporate/business/professional market simultaneously from three directions. First, we are exploring distribution agreements with major manufacturers, specifically Apple and Bell & Howell upon whose equipment (Apple II Plus) Cdex programs initially run. Second, Cdex will expand its direct, corporate sales effort with the addition of senior salespeople once financing is completed. And third, the first Cdex Training Center will open in the heart of Silicon Valley (Sunnyvale, California) by mid-1983.

We feel a multifaceted approach is desirable if Cdex is to capture the high ground of being the first successful electronic publisher of quality computer-assisted, human resource development materials.

5. Sufficient financing to achieve a critical mass of material and market recognition relatively quickly. The microcomputer revolution is bringing with it a flood of single purpose, program writers/producers. These software people are vital to the growth of the microcomputer market, and in time Cdex will publish and market certain of their works. At the same time, major traditional publishers (McGraw-Hill, Addison-

Wesley, etc.) are busy thinking about ways they, too, can capitalize on the technological revolution, and their distribution networks are of interest to Cdex for its products. Both of the above are going on while the manufacturers are spending money to stimulate primary demand. This all adds up to the fact that we are in the very early, confused, startup stage of a new industry.

Money ($500,000) is needed by Cdex to bring on board the small team of top people who can systematically exploit the confusion (authors, manufacturers, distribution systems, market segments) in the construction of a new kind of company, the Cdex electronic publishing company. How the money will be used and the "systematic exploitation" is covered in detail in the balance of this business plan.

II. OBJECTIVES

Overall, the Cdex management intends to build an unusually profitable $100 million company by 1990. We are confident we can do so because a) the basic market for human resource development materials is growing rapidly and will continue to do so around the world, b) we have proprietary technology in our material preparation, and c) we expect the microcomputer revolution to provide us with delivery devices in every nook and cranny of society. In this latter regard, we will follow along behind wherever the micros are sold and used, not lead the way. More specifically, our projected profit statements for the first five years are shown below.

In summary, the primary Cdex corporate objectives are as follows:

1. Achieve $100 million in sales volume (1980 dollars) by 1990 with a minimum NPBT of 25 percent.
2. Maintain an ROE exceeding 30 percent throughout the history of the company. (See balance sheets later in the business plan.)
3. Be included in the top five names mentioned in any post-1983 survey of industry-knowledgeable people who influence corporate/professional thinking on microcomputer/communications/human resource development technology.

CDEX PROFIT PROJECTION 1982-1986

Legend:
CU = Cdex Unit
DISK = Programs
TC = Training Centers
C OF GS = Cost of Goods Sold
CORP DIV = Corporate Div
TC DIV = Training Center Div
G&A = General and Administrative
DEPRCN = Depreciation
CP EQ = Capital Equipment

YEAR →	1982	1983	1984	1985	1986
# OF CU'S SOLD	39450	130500	675000	1575000	3437500
# OF DISKS SHIPPED	5000	10000	25000	50000	75000
# OF TC'S	1	2	3	5	8
# OF EMPLOYEES	22	50	100	250	400
SALES	1190850	5721525	20522250	41580000	73077000
C OF GS	119085	858229	4104450	10395000	18269250
GROSS MAR	1071765	4863296	16417800	31185000	54807750
GM%	90	85	80	75	75
CORP DIV EXP	253258	1081160	3851760	6595320	11581040
EXP%SLS	21	19	19	16	16
TC DIV EXP	158665	406275	752680	1273433	2046132
EXP%SLS	13	7	4	3	3
BOTH DIV %SLS	35	26	22	19	19
G & A	595483	949125	1081773	1519679	2086785
%SLS	50	17	5	4	3
DEPRCN 20% CP EQ	6000	16000	36000	66000	200000
INCENTIVE COMP	0	286076	1026113	2079000	3653850
NPBT	58359	2124660	9669474	19651568	35239943
TAXES	20000	1000000	4500000	9000000	15500000
NPAT	38359	1124660	5169474	10651568	19739943
ROE	8	225	1034	—	—
ROI (CUMM CSH =1)	21	119	114	75	67
ROS	2	20	25	26	27

III. MARKET ANALYSIS

The total United States market for microcomputer programs is currently considered to be in the $50–80 million class. This annual figure includes programs containing games, personal applications, and business applications. This software market is expected to grow at 40 percent a year for the foreseeable future in parallel with the microcomputer hardware market.

As mentioned earlier, the thrust of much of the new software produced in the years ahead will be toward business applications—particularly applications based on accounting information. For example, the August 1981 full page announcements in major newspapers by both IBM and HP stressed the accounting type applications of their "personal" computers . . . i.e., their micros. Few people/companies are prepared today to provide nonaccounting-type programs. Bell & Howell is one such company by virtue of PASS, its Professional Authoring Software System. Cdex has already licensed PASS from B&H. More on this later.

Deltak, a leading company in the training of computer people for companies, is the only known company that at this time appears to share Cdex's vision of the opportunity ahead. Deltak has historically used standup seminars and videotapes for their training programs. They too have become a PASS licensee, and they have recently started advertising their "Microvision" programs which run as Cdex's do—on Apple II Plus machines, Deltak is a ten-year-old, worldwide company with sales in excess of $50 million. Exhibit 2 contains one of their brochures. Deltak, a venture capital funded startup, was sold recently to Prentice-Hall.

In summary to this point, Cdex will sell in the wake of the obvious, accounting oriented programs which are proliferating in the marketplace. For example, we expect that most of our customers in 1982 and 1983 will already own the necessary microcomputer hardware. Over the longer run, when the market is viewed strictly in terms of microcomputer programs, Cdex expects in 1987 to be selling 5 to 10 percent of a billion dollar a year, packaged software market.

A different and more useful way to evaluate the Cdex market opportunity is to look at the money being spent on business and professional development. The American Society for Training & Development (ASTD) estimates that the total market for commercial training and development materials (seminars, books, films, posters, site costs, speakers, etc.) exceeded $1 billion in 1980. This figure does not include the money spent for the continuing education of legal, medical, and accounting practitioners. Supervisory training packages alone (one of Cdex's major product areas) are selling at a rate of over $25 million per year through a variety of suppliers, including Louis Allen, Scientific Methods, Sterling, Kepner Tregoe, BNA, CRM, and Dartnell. Cdex is interested primarily in publishing computer-assisted materials for executives, managers, supervisors, and salespeople—the subsegments that are historically the most popular targets for packaged development materials. In 1980, U.S. corporations are estimated to have spent well over $200 million on commercial products, seminars, and services for these four subsegments.

While a down economy can have a dampening effect in any given year, this chosen group of four subsegments is expected to expand at an average rate of 20 percent a year without the application of microcomputer technology. Cdex management believes that its technology might add 5 percent to the natural growth rate. The end result is annual markets as follows (1980 dollars):

	$ Market	Cdex Share	$ Sales
1982	200 M	1%	2.7
1983	250	9	24
1984	310	12	37
1985	390	13	52
1986	488	14	70

In summary, Cdex will operate in a market defined by the intersection of two distinct trend lines. The first is the spread of microcomputer technology. That technology breeds a software vacuum which Cdex, as an electronic publisher, will attempt to fill. The total market for microcomputer programs in 1987 is estimated to be $1 billion. The second trend of interest is the increase in management and salespeople development, with an eye toward improved productivity. Cdex has a very favorable benefit-to-cost product story to sell into this market, which is estimated to be at least $.5 billion in 1987 ($488 million in 1986—see table above).

Of the $1 billion (1987) microcomputer software market, an educated guess is that two thirds will be bought for business and professional applications ($660M). Of the $660M, perhaps 30 percent ($200M) will be for human resource development rather than accounting-related uses. Cdex expects to own 30–40 percent of that $200M market segment in 1987. The situation is summarized graphically below.

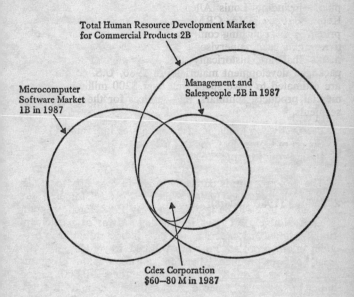

Total Human Resource Development Market for Commercial Products 2B

Microcomputer Software Market 1B in 1987

Management and Salespeople .5B in 1987

Cdex Corporation $60–80 M in 1987

IV. PRODUCTION

There are six basic steps in the production process:

1. Capture quality subject matter on selected subjects
2. Program design
3. Program writing
4. Transfer of completed program into computer form (onto floppy disks)
5. Program validation
6. Program security, duplication, and distribution mechanics

Based on our experience to date in the production of high-quality Cdex programs, the allocation of time across the above is as follows:

1. 10% Subject matter acquisition
2. 10% Design
3. 50% Writing
4. 20% Programming
5. 5% Validation
6. 5% Mechanics
   _____
   100%

So far we have produced four programs:

XYZ Company Planning Process (fictitious company name)
Perspective on Managing (#1 in catalog in Exhibit 1)
Stages of Company Growth (#2)
Basic Profit Math (#26)

The first program is currently in use in over fifty locations in the United States. The last three are the basis for the Cdex sales effort that will be initiated in early 1982. Each program is approximately an hour in length in terms of participant running time. Our experience to date indicates that each program in our proprietary library will take us roughly 600–800 total hours to produce. Therefore, the forty initial programs planned (see Exhibit 1) will require over 20,000 person hours to complete. Once a master disk is completed for a given program, additional disks (copies) will cost Cdex under $50 each (direct cost) for duplication and shipping.

The Cdex production process is dependent upon the PASS (Professional Authoring Software System) authoring program which we have licensed from Bell & Howell. The program enables Cdex authors to program quickly and efficiently —once the subject material is in a structured, interactive format. Cdex is also licensed to resell copies of PASS to corporate customers interested in creating their own programs.

Bell & Howell currently has fifteen direct salespeople in the field selling PASS plus B&H microcomputers (private labeled from Apple). The activities of B&H are expected to be a plus for Cdex—both from a marketing and a production standpoint. In effect, B&H's success in the field will create a demand for Cdex proprietary programs. In addition, B&H's programming expertise will be of value to Cdex in such esoteric matters as encoding programs to prevent unauthorized duplication. Apple is also expected to be of help on this matter. To date, B&H's PASS customers include General Motors, Firemen's Fund, Standard Oil of California, and Westinghouse, to name a few.

Up to this point in time, Cdex has made the necessary capital expenditures to equip two programmers:

PASS License $30,000
Microcomputers (2) $10,000
Miscellaneous Equipment $5000

Over the next two years Cdex management expects to spend no more than $100,000 in total on office and program production capital expenditures. The production of proprietary Cdex programs is not capital intensive. The Cdex "secret" is in the conversion process, i.e., in capturing quality subject matter—proven subject matter—and converting it via learning and computer technology into a new form, namely colorful, computer-assisted, interactive, interesting, multimedia instruction. Two members of the Cdex management and programming team are estimated to be among the 100 most experienced people in the world in this conversion process insofar as it has been applied to more conceptual subjects such as those for management and salespeople development. (Most of the remaining 100 are with Control Data Corporation which has developed the PLATO system of interactive training using a CD main-frame computer.)

Knowledge of and skill in the conversion process (adaptation and reformating of conceptual material) is relatively rare, and it lies at the heart of Cdex management's decision to position the company as an electronic *publisher* . . . rather than as a software producer of original material or a management training house. Within five to seven years, we expect to have 500–1000 individual titles in our library covering a range of subjects of interest to "knowledge workers" (Peter Drucker's term) in the business and professional market.

From a staffing standpoint, program production will be concentrated in our Program Development Division (PDD) which will operate as a profit center after year two. We expect to have approximately nine programmers employed by

1983 with at least half of them working at home on Cdex supplied microcomputers. Currently Cdex has one programmer full-time and another on call, a staffing level adequate to our current level of startup operation.

In general, we will develop our own programmers. We will use essentially the same approach for developing a core of three to four learning technologists—the people who must work in front of the programmers to break the subject (whatever it is) into an interesting, digestible, logically-sequenced series of frames with appropriate questions and responses and branches to insure learning. Cdex currently has the learning technologist on its staff for its initial library. By 1983, we will have broadened our staff as necessary to handle new authors.

Currently Cdex management plans to approach a select group of proven authors to arrange for exclusive rights to the use of their materials in the Cdex computer-assisted format. Included in that group are:

(Names will be provided to serious prospective investors on request.)

Approaches to these authors will begin once Cdex financing is completed. We expect to operate on a royalty basis with signed authors, but on occasion may have to put some money "up front." In some respects Cdex will resemble a Twentieth-Century Fox which negotiates with authors for movie rights (different format) to certain proven books (e.g., *Superman*).

In summary, the forty planned programs in the initial Cdex library are thought to be a relatively low risk venture that will carry the company to well over a third of the way to the $100 million sales mark by 1990. Additional authors on additional proven topics (from setting up quality circles and EEO guidelines to decision making and working with Discounted Cash Flow) will be added systematically. In every case, Cdex will be utilizing a known and understood production process that reflects a unique, modern, relatively proprietary (Bell & Howell, Control Data, Deltak, and Cdex) combination of learning and computer technologies. Cdex will be the premier electronic publisher of human resource development products.

V. MARKETING

Smart marketing is the matter to which the Cdex top management [chief executive officer (CEO), chief operating officer (COO)] and board have given the most concentrated attention in the last few months. We believe we have developed a cost effective approach to the embryonic marketplace. IBM and HP's Fall 1981 entries into the corporate market for personal computers tends to verify our line of thinking which can be summarized as follows:

> *Cdex will sell improved productivity, more effective management and salesmanship, and enhanced computer literacy to progressive United States companies via both direct sales effort and Cdex Training Centers in high density markets.*

In general, our line of products will complement the efforts by Apple, TI, Radio Shack, Bell & Howell, HP, and IBM to sell personal computers. In general, our competition is the older, established purveyors of traditional human resource development products such as AMA (American Management Association), Louis Allen, Scientific Methods (Grid), industrial film companies like BNA and Roundtable, and the wave of seminar companies that have sprung up in recent years. In general, we will sell on a cost/benefit justification basis that contrasts the Cdex method of producing desired results with the alternatives. And in general, at least in the early years, we will sell a premium-priced product primarily to corporations rather than individuals. Details follow.

Product positioning. We identified twelve discrete positions around which we could weave our marketing effort. They were as follows. Cdex early products could be promoted as:

1. Computer-assisted management and sales effectiveness improvers
2. Continuing education programs
3. A single, integrated—top management to supervisors—management development program
4. An MBA program for in-house use

5. A tested supervisory training program (There are currently 400 corporate users of the contents of Cdex programs numbered 11 through 20. See Exhibit 1.)
6. Basic ingredients for developing a "corporate culture," a phrase increasingly used in business circles
7. A strategic planning or strategic management series
8. Computer literacy enhancer (Provide a comfortable way for companies to introduce computers to their people.)
9. Productivity (or profitability) improvers
10. Building block materials to supplement in-house development activities
11. Follow-on materials to live seminars based on Cdex products
12. Computer software

Given our pricing plans and our interest in developing a firm hold on the corporate market (see later), we have decided to position Cdex products as:

9. Productivity improvers
1. Computer-assisted management and sales effectiveness improvers
8. Computer literacy enhancers

As a practical matter, we will also use #10 (building blocks to supplement in-house efforts) as necessary—particularly when calling on corporate training directors. Alternatives #2, 3, 5, and 11 were passed as primary approaches because they led us toward becoming too subject matter oriented. Also, these options lacked pizzazz. Alternatives #4, 6, and 7 were not, strictly speaking, technically complete, and the Cdex programs involved would not, by themselves, produce the results implied. Alternative #12 would carry us into a morass of low-priced, undifferentiated products that will be coming onto the market.

Our sense is that productivity and effectiveness are powerful, current themes for the corporate world, and they tie in with our plan to show that Cdex products are superior on a cost/benefit basis. Our sense is also that the personal computer publicity boom is going to create a demand for computer literacy to which Cdex's nonaccounting-oriented materials are a perfect answer.

Market segments. We identified eleven discrete segments Cdex could pursue by various means. They were:

1. Fortune 1000 companies with established training budgets (Both the Cdex CEO and potential COO have reasonably good access to these companies.)
2. Smaller, technology-based, growth-oriented companies—many of which already own personal computers
3. Bell & Howell customers (B&H has sold over $20 million of microcomputers upon which Cdex programs will run.)
4. Apple Computer customers (Cdex programs run on Apple II Plus machines. There are 50,000 now in use.)
5. Training centers (Companies send individual managers, supervisors, or sales people to a nearby center.)
6. Individual consumers—typically people who already own personal computers
7. Selected vertical segments such as high-tech companies, banks, or retailing establishments
8. The professions, i.e., accounting, law, medicine, nursing
9. Government
10. Commercial schools, e.g., technician training, AMA, nontraditional MBA programs, etc.
11. Universities and colleges

Our thinking is that over the longer term, Cdex wants to be well established as *the* electronic publisher with a well-oiled distribution network to corporations. This point of view reflects the Cdex management team's interest, experience, and belief about where profit opportunity lies in the years ahead. Therefore, we have selected our segments accordingly with one proviso: We will concentrate on a geographic roll out (a form of segmentation) starting with west coast companies that are one or more of the following:

1. Fortune 1000
2. Smaller, growth companies
3. Bell & Howell customers
4. Apple Computer customers

In addition, we will establish a Cdex Training Center in the geographic heart of Silicon Valley to which interested corporate customers can send individuals to take Cdex programs on a one-at-a-time basis. So add:

5. Training Centers

The other six segments have been rejected for the foreseeable future for a variety of reasons that will not be reviewed here.
In summary, our targeted market is as follows:

I. Human resource development for productivity and effectiveness
   A. Business and professional "knowledge workers"
      1. Corporate purchases—primarily manufacturers
         a. Large and higher growth companies that reside in high population density areas
            i. West Coast—NY/Boston—Atlanta—DFW —Houston

And we will solicit these targeted segments via direct sales efforts and Cdex Training Centers.

Product features. Cdex management feels that Cdex programs, used singly or in a series (see the matrix in Exhibit 1), offer the following, quantifiable benefits to corporate users:

1. Ease of administration. Programs are not instructor-dependent and can be used/scheduled twenty-four hours a day in one or more locations. In short, the programs are *need driven* . . . as opposed to schedule driven.

2. Consistent quality. With a Cdex program, management knows precisely what each participant gets—today, tomorrow, and beyond . . . in every part of the company. All members of the management or sales team, therefore, can sing from the same sheet of music, so to speak.

3. Consistent message. The people promoted or hired next week (month, year) get the same basic instruction that their predecessors did. This is the basis for synergism in a company.

4. Low cost per person, per program. For any repetitive development need, Cdex will be less expensive than *any* alternative (meetings, manuals, memos, off-site seminars, etc.). Cdex is aiming at a $10/person/program objective by its fifth year. (See Pricing later.)

5. Superior subject recall and application. The benefits of the Cdex methodology were covered in Section I.

6. Flexibility. Cdex self-instructional programs can be integrated with virtually any other human resource development approach. For example, a sequence of Cdex programs can be periodically reviewed on a group basis. An instructor (or, better yet, a line manager) using a Cdex Review Session Leader's Guide can lead a provocative review session based on the material in the program.

7. Technology interface. To the extent that "the medium is the message," companies using personal computers to upgrade their people are conveying an upbeat, on-top-of-it image for the eighties.

8. Pedigreed material. Each subject in the Cdex library is based, once again, on proven material, i.e., it has worked in the field. Cdex pulls together the best from academia and the real world of actual practice.

The details of precisely how these features will be fabricated into selling aids and advertising/promotion material will be worked out as the scheduled marketing talent is added to the Cdex team.

Pricing. Cdex management has examined in depth two major issues regarding pricing. First was whether to sell programs outright or license them for specific time periods (like a year) as a small gesture to keep control of the material. Second was whether to sell programs for a fixed figure or to sell them on a per-participant basis. Our conclusion is that we should sell them outright (rather than license them), and that we should sell them outright on the basis of the possible number of users in the buying organization.

Our long-term objective is to arrive at a point where we can sell programs based on a $10-per-participant, per-program basis. One participant taking one program is equivalent to what we call one Cdex Unit (1 CU). Roughly, our pricing schedule for 1982 through 1984 is as follows:

1982	1984
$29/CU	$25/CU

Here is how the planned pricing will work. If Company X has 900 people in supervision and management and plans to buy the 10-program supervisory training series, the total price in 1982 would be $29 \times 900 \times 10 = \$261,000$. For this figure, Cdex would provide ten complete personal computers and ten copies of each of the ten programs . . . so Company X would have the equivalent of ten complete training "stations." (In 1982, we will provide one station for each $25,000 purchase . . . or give credit to those who already own the necessary equipment.)

Another example, Company Y has forty salespeople and wishes to purchase five Cdex programs.

$$\$29 \times 40 \times 5 = \$5,800$$

We would provide no hardware in this instance.

We recognize the weakness in this per-participant approach, namely trying to get a fair initial price. It may be that we will have to establish a minimum price per program. A figure between $1,500 and $1,900 is being discussed by the Cdex board.

Sales. We are currently executing the second of a four-phase sales effort. Phase I took place between April and October of 1981 during which time the Cdex CEO exposed (in a non-selling mode) the first four completed programs to approximately 300 decision makers. Two hundred were in a local executive continuing education program; the other 100 were potential customers or investors, or both. The overwhelming response was positive interest that far exceeded mere curiosity. This business plan reflects much of the feedback received. Approximately $30,000 in sales were generated during this period.

Phase II, a direct personal selling effort by the CEO and potential chief operating officer (COO), was launched in mid-November and is aimed at signing on at least one major customer who will, in part, dictate which programs in the initial Cdex library will be produced next. We are quoting a figure of $10,000 per program (one-time charge) for which the customer receives programs featuring the buying company's name in the title (cosmetic customizing) plus publicity.

Phase III will begin with the addition of the COO full-time at which point he will simultaneously a) seek additional major customers to help us complete the library, b) recruit vice-presidents for the Corporate and Cdex Training Center Divisions (we have candidates identified for each position), and c) initiate our campaign to add at least two key authors to the Cdex stable.

Phase IV will commence in the third or fourth quarter of 1982, approximately three months after the vice-presidents are on board and oriented. Phase IV will consist of a coordinated direct selling effort in a specific region (probably northern or southern California) to sell both Cdex programs and/or utilization of the local Cdex Training Center.

Note: Our current thinking is that corporations will be charged a price of $35–$39 per person, per program (1 CU) for people scheduled into our Training Center. This is a 25 percent premium over the "buy" price, but it allows companies to keep their human resource development cost on a variable cost basis. This may be important if the economy continues to undulate.

As a result of our systematic selling effort, we plan to sell Cdex Units as follows:

Year	Sales—CU's
1982	40,650
1983	165,500
1984	720,000
1985	1,657,500
1986	3,605,500

Both the sales and pricing expectations are shown in graph form below.

In conclusion, the Cdex marketing effort has been formulated from the best information and advice reasonably available plus the extensive experience base of the board. Further refinements will be incorporated as we expand our base of direct field selling. We are well aware that program distribution is now a major challenge confronting the entire microcomputer industry. Cdex intends to be a leader in developing a profitable, pacesetting solution.

VI. ORGANIZATION

Work is well along to bring together a core of qualified, capable, interested people to build the company described in this plan. Almost since its conception, Cdex has had an active board. The CEO and COO (committed candidate) have been

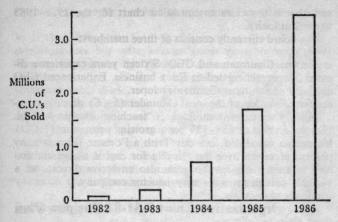

1 C.U. = 1 Cdex Unit = 1 person taking 1 program

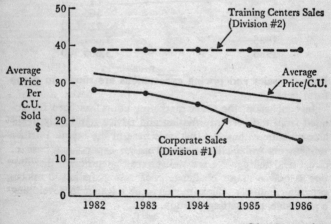

Cdex Corporation

working together since June 1981 in collaboration on both operations and the development of this plan. The program production effort has gone smoothly due to the tenacity of our senior programmer. And candidates are in mind for both vice-president slots: Corporate Division and Training Center Division.

Below is the Cdex organization chart for the 1982–1983 period (at least).

The board currently consists of three members:

Brown: Chairman and CEO. Sixteen years experience directly related to Cdex business. Experienced CEO and management developer.

Smith: Venture Capitalist. Founder (1965) of early company in multimedia, "teaching machine" field. Wide experience with growing companies.

Jones: Currently an officer with a Fortune 100 company where he is responsible for capital budgeting and strategic planning. Is also an active director of a high growth semiconductor company.

CDEX Organization Chart 9-31-81 Business Plan

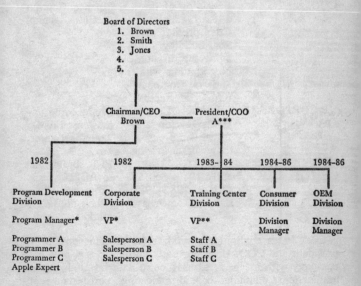

*Candidate identified
**Candidate interviewed
***Candidate committed

The chart above outlines the basic concept for the development of Cdex. In practice, the management team will operate as a functional team with a single profit center through 1982 and into 1983.

The management team currently consists of two people. Once the needed capital is committed, two additional line people will be added. This group of four is expected to suffice through 1982. In 1983, at least one functional officer (e.g., CFO or Controller) may be added. At a later point in time, managers for two additional divisions (Consumer Division and OEM Division) will be considered.

The management positions (1981–1983):

Title/Name	Primary Responsibility	Secondary
CEO/Brown	Execution of this plan. Staffing + team building. Development of Cdex library of programs.	Marketing.
COO/A	Execution of the 1982–1983 plan. Cdex profitability. Staff building. Managing the divisions. Negotiations with authors. Computer mfgrs. interface.	Finance. Communications technology.
VP-CORPORATE DIV	Sell 40K CUs in 1982. Develop salesforce. Build customer base. Pricing.	Product line extensions. Build Training Center Div.
VP-TRAINING CENTER DIV.	Open TC #1 by early 1983. Sell 5K CUs in 1982–1983. Build customer base.	P. R. Build links to ASTD. Assist Corporate Div. Assess consumer market.

Cdex has a committed candidate (A) for the position of president and COO. He is currently an officer of a blue chip company with extensive experience in data processing, communications, planning, capital budgeting, performance appraisal (of line managers), and corporate negotiations. He has a strong line management background which includes five years as president of a small computer company and ten years as a SVP of a major bank. He has participated fully in the preparation of this plan. A is forty-four years old and has a degree in physics as well as an MBA.

Cdex has active candidates for both the vice-president slots. The candidate for the Corporate Division is currently a senior account executive for a $100 million, New York-based, service company. She has a very, very strong record of success in selling to major companies. She is thirty-six and has a BS in engineering.

The candidate for VP, Training Center Division, is currently the vice-president of marketing for a $30 million consumer products company in the Bay Area. He has a broad base of marketing and sales experience running back to three years with P & G in the 1960s. He also has a sound background in general management having spent five years in charge of two different smaller companies. This candidate is forty and has a BA and an MBA. (Resumes of the management team (CEO, COO, and one VP candidate) are included in Exhibit 3.)

There are two other key positions unique to Cdex that will require qualified people in the 1982–1983 timeframe.

Director, Program Production:
  Primary responsibility will be to manage all aspects of the microcomputer and software development interface. This person will have computer expertise.
Director, Programming:
  Primary responsibility will be the application of modern learning technology to business, human resource development opportunities. This person will have learning technology expertise as well as microcomputer experience.

We expect to be able to attract experienced people from the Bay Area to fill these positions.

Generally speaking, other than for the COO (and possibly one of the VP's), staffing for Cdex will be drawn from near the corporate headquarters.

Long-run Outlook   Following is a *rough* word picture of how Cdex is expected to look by about 1988–1989. At that point in time the company will have five profit centers and annual sales in excess of $70 million.

Corporate Division   Sells Cdex products plus some others directly to corporations. Has forty to fifty direct sales people in field working out of five to six regional offices in the

United States plus offices in London, Mexico City, and Hong Kong. The Cdex name is well known and respected in the corporate world. We are doing image advertising in the *Wall Street Journal*. Sales average $1,000,000 per salesperson per year. Total Sales = $40M; Gross Margin = 75 percent.

Training Center Division Has twelve training centers in high density areas of the United States plus one in Mexico City (with fifty training rooms). Each center averages $1M sales per year . . . operating at about 65 percent of capacity. Center's are open ten to twelve hours a day. Total sales = $13M; Gross Margin = 90 percent.

Program Development Division Primary responsibility-preparation and QC of Cdex programs. In addition, PDD takes on selective "custom programming" contracts . . . particularly when they are on generic subjects that can be packaged by Cdex for its proprietary library. Total Sales = $15M; Gross Margin = 40 percent.

Consumer Division Sells Cdex products plus some others directly to small business people and consumers via a variety of methods. Has four, pilot learning centers in shopping centers in NY, LA, Palo Alto, and Washington, D.C. Total Sales = $20M; Gross Margin = 60 percent.

Original Equipment Division Sells Cdex products through microcomputer manufacturers. Total Sales = $6M; Gross Margin = 15 percent—much too low. But Cdex position here keeps company at forefront of continuing personal computer revolution.

VII. FINANCIALS

Since June 1981 management has developed several computer models of Cdex in an attempt to develop a realistic picture of the funding needs and performance of the company in the years ahead. We have settled on best case and worst case (most conservative) scenarios with 1982 shown by month, 1983 by quarters, and 1984–1986 by years. These two very detailed scenarios are in our computer and available for examination, explanation, and discussion to interested management team candidates and investors. The key numbers from the projections look like this (in millions):

Best Case	1982	1983	1984	1985	1986
Sales $	1.2	5.7	20.5	41.6	73.1
NPAT $	.04	1.1	5.2	10.6	19.7
ROS %*	3	20	25	26	27
Cumm Cash $	.18	.9	4.5	14.1	29.3
Worst Case					
Sales $	.4	1.5	2.9	4.3	7.5
NPAT $	(.1)	.2	.5	.8	1.7
ROS %	—	11	18	19	23
Cumm Cash $	.2	.2	.7	1.4	3.0

* ROS % = Return on Sales percentage

In reviewing these two cases, we offer several observations. First, there is a big difference between the two scenarios . . . insofar as the top lines (sales) goes. But it is our considered opinion that with precisely the right packaging and marketing of our library, Cdex can indeed fulfill its opportunity very quickly. It can catch on and explode along with the microcomputer business. On the other hand, training materials per se are historically not "exploders," and our intended, rational, cost/benefit sell can take time. The front-end investment ($300,000–500,000) is roughly the same in either case, and the returns (on sales, investment, and equity) are *very* attractive in both scenarios . . . as a discussion of our detailed, line itemed budgets with interested parties will show. Cdex management is confident it can successfully pilot the company on an opportunistic course between the two extremes, with the Best Case being the more likely outcome.

A second observation is that Cdex is a high-margin business that holds promise of being essentially self funding once it is launched. The cost of goods sold is minimal; inventory requirements are relatively small; capital investments will be primarily for microcomputer equipment (as opposed to bricks and mortar); and the programming expense structure is highly variable in that it can be increased or decreased incrementally as necessary. This gives management a lot of flexibility to deal with the changing times.

A third observation is that the intrinsic value of the company does not show in the financial projections (particularly the balance sheets) because it is in the finished programs—a growing library of sophisticated, computer-assisted, development programs covering the great ideas in business management and selling. The true value of the programs will not be reflected in the inventory figures. This library, and therefore, Cdex, is expected to become a very saleable asset to a host of potential buyers ranging from traditional publishers to computer manufacturers and the new world of TV networks. This means it will be practical for investors to recoup their money with appropriate capital gains within a reasonable time period of four to six years.

A final observation is that the basic idea behind Cdex is readily expandable. Broader coverage of the corporate market, foreign language versions of our programs, more training centers, and new subject areas for the library are all extensions of the efforts outlined in this Business Plan.

In summary, we have detailed plans reflecting pricing, sales effort, staffing, production, and capital expenditures for Cdex. The management expects to aim for the best case and be alert to the need to proceed on the basis of the worst case scenario. Since the company's inception in mid-1981, the Cdex management has consistently met its plans at each step along the way. With the necessary funding and staff additions, it will continue to do so.

The current (1/82) balance sheet of the company is approximately as follows:

Cash	$ 20,000	A/P	$ 5,000
A/R	0		
Fixed Assets	20,000	Debt	13,000
Programs (3)	150,000	Net Worth	172,000
	$190,000		$190,000

VIII. OWNERSHIP

This business plan provides the basis for the third round of financing for Cdex. The history of the financing of the company is as follows:

History	# Shares		Ave. $/Share	% Cdex	$ Cash Invested
Round I—June 1981					
Brown	1,400,000	Common	.04*	100	$56,000

Round II—Sept. 1981

| Directors | 65,000 Common | .50 | 4 | $32,500 |

Round III—Current

| Investors | 650,000 C. Pfd. | .78 | 30 | $500,000 |

*Plus all electronic publishing rights to the forty programs shown in Exhibit 1

Summary Including Management Stock Options (COO and VP's):

Brown	1,400,000	54
Directors	65,000	3
Investors	650,000	25
Mgmt. Stock Options	485,000	18
	2,600,000	100%

At this time we wish to sell 650,000 shares of preferred stock that is convertible 1:1 into common stock. The offering price for the convertible preferred is $.78.

Exhibits

Cdex Corporation
Business Plan

Exhibit 1

The Cdex
Personal Computer
Library

Answers to 7 Important Questions

1 What is the Cdex Library?
The Cdex Library is a collection of high quality, English language personal computer programs on managing and selling practices. The first programs in the Library were available to users in June, 1981. Additional programs are being added each month. All of the programs run on Apple personal computers.

2 What specific subjects are available?
Thirty of the initial forty programs deal with subjects of current importance to executives, managers, and supervisors in dynamic companies. Ten of the forty are on industrial selling subjects. Each program is designed to bring together the best *proven* material from leading business schools and from the real world of actual practice. The enclosed matrix shows the forty titles classified in ten major series.

3 Why use Cdex programs in your company?
There's a famous saying that goes like this: "I know that half the money I spend on management development is wasted . . . but I don't know which half!" Cdex programs mold learning and computer technology into interactive, personal development experiences that essentially guarantee the application of the subject matter on the job. When *quality* subject matter is remembered and applied, much of the "half wasted" disappears. And since Cdex programs are self-instructional, self-pacing, and portable, they can be used when and where they are needed . . . either individually or as part of an instructor-led development effort. Cdex programs

are building blocks that can be configured to meet your specific needs.

4 What are the costs involved?
Generally speaking, program costs are a function of the number of users in your company. For example, a company with 100 people in management and supervision would pay approximately $2900 to purchase or license a Cdex program. Hardware costs for the required Apple II Plus computer; one 33 Disk Drive; and one color monitor are between $3000 and $4000. Cdex will provide the hardware free-of-charge to major Library users.

5 What support services does Cdex provide?
When a series of programs are purchased or licensed, Cdex will train your company's training coordinator at no additional cost. Cdex can also provide the PASS (Professional Authoring Software System) program and assistance if you wish to prepare custom, computer-assisted development programs in your own company.

6 Who are the Cdex authors?
Contracts have been and are being made with recognized experts in subjects important to companies on the go in the 1980's.

For example, along with other programs, the core series of programs on strategic planning shown in the attached matrix are authored by Professor Steven C. Brandt of the Stanford Business School and are based on his new book, *Strategic Planning in Emerging Companies.*

7 What next?
Personally sample the programs of interest. Then select for use in your company the configuration of materials that will give you the maximum payoff in the coming year.

Contact Cdex for assistance in bringing the new world of computer-assisted human resource development to your company.

Cdex Corporation

EXHIBIT 1

**The Cdex
Personal Computer
Library**

1. **Perspective on Managing**— Managing vs. doing. How to study, improve and use managing practices appropriate to your level of responsibility.

2. **Stages of Company Growth** —Five major stages of growth and the associated crisis at each stage. How to handle each crisis.

3. **Setting Company Objectives**—Criteria for sound objectives. Areas in which objectives should be set. MBO pitfalls to avoid.

4. **Selecting Planning Units**— Why planning units are necessary in a company of any complexity. Criteria for units. How proper units facilitate a planning process.

5. **Managing the Planning Process**—Key ingredients to making plans that get implemented. How to avoid the once-a-year project syndrome.

6. **Selecting a Planning Technique**—Eight major planning techniques. How to pick and stick with the best one for your company.

7. **Basic Strategies for Building a Company**—Six generic, proven ways to grow an enterprise and the minimum requirements for success for each strategy.

8. **Organizational Structures for Building a Company**— Four basic structures (func-tional to matrix) for carrying out a company strategy. Pitfalls to avoid in changing your structure.

9. **Productivity Fundamentals** —Methods improvements. Involving all your people. How to work smarter, not harder, in the 1980's.

10. **Cultivating a Corporate Culture**—Importance of a common vocabulary, company rituals, and the various reward systems. How to internalize values that enhance plan implementation.

11. **Perspective on Supervising** —Supervising vs. doing. How to break old habits of individual success and start achieving planned results through others.

12. **Setting Your Objectives**— Monthly, quarterly, and longer-term objectives. Criteria for sound objectives. Areas in which to set objectives.

13. **Improving Productivity**— Locating improvement possibilities. Use of checklists. Involving others. Selling methods improvements up the line.

14. **Working with Individuals** —Why general rules don't work. How people differ. Recent trends in social values. Dealing successfully with individual differences.

15. **Solving Day-To-Day Problems**—Kinds of problems

you face. Sources of problems. Sources of solutions. A procedure for getting the best solutions.

16. **Giving Day-To-Day Instructions**—Problems you face in communicating. When to use oral and written instructions. How to get the results you want.

17. **Training Your People**—Common pitfalls to avoid. Problems new employees face. How to develop effective training experiences.

18. **Disciplining Your People**—Basic principles. Special issues of the times. How to discipline without trepidation.

19. **Delegating with Confidence**—Reasons managers and supervisors delegate poorly. Psychological hurdles to overcome. How to get the delegating habit.

20. **Questioning & Listening**—Basic types of questions and when to use them. How to listen with your whole self. Drawing the most out of your people.

21. **Motivating Your People**—Factors that motivate people and how those factors change. What motivates people today. How to "unlock" each of your people individually.

22. **Evaluating Individual Performance**—Measuring activity, effort, appearances, and results. How to let people know how they are doing.

23. **Counseling Your People**—Problems people face. Signals to recognize. When to take action. How to help your people help themselves.

24. **Building a Career in Managing**—Factors for continuing success. Understanding managing. Setting realistic personal objectives. How to realize your ambitions.

25. **Planning Your Time**—Major time sumps. Setting priorities. Sticking with priorities. How to allocate your energies for maximum impact.

26. **Basic Profit Math**—A graphic approach that integrates marketing, production, and accounting. Break-even analysis. Effect of changing product mix. How to use BPM in planning.

27. **Ten Commandments for Growing a Company**—Key, proven principles for managing startups and young companies. Author is experienced entrepreneur and executive.

28. **Guide to Writing a Business Plan**—Concept, market opportunity, production, marketing, people, cash flow, and ownership. How to present your idea to investors.

29. **Developing a Competitive Advantage**—Four basic ways to excell in a chosen marketplace. How to cultivate your proprietary edge.

30. **Evaluating Company Performance**—Range of evaluation techniques: EPS, ROS, ROI, ROE, etc. Key

Exhibit 1

factors to consider.

31. **Analyzing a Territory—** Key components for profitable growth. Getting the picture on competition. How to reach strategic conclusions.

32. **Working with Customers—** Why generalizations are dangerous. How people differ. Pressures customers face. How to tailor your approach to individual differences.

33. **Questioning & Listening to Sell—**Do you talk too much? Three basic types of questions. Maximizing the input from your customers.

34. **Selling in Writing—**When to use oral and written communications. Writing pitfalls to avoid. How to make your point on paper.

35. **Selling with Proposals—** Specifying the need. Laying out your solution. Formating. Action language. Closing. Followup.

36. **Thinking Creatively—**Selling solutions vs. selling products or services. Opening your mind. Opening the minds of others. Getting your message across.

37. **Understanding Profit Math** —Where sales dollars go. Product mix. Pricing. How to enhance your reputation as a businessperson.

38. **Setting Call Objectives—** Identifying the results you want. Analyzing the customer. What are the values involved? How to maximize your ROE (Return on Energy) each day.

39. **Conducting Group Meetings—**Setting objectives. Identifying the decision makers. Agendas. Presentation techniques. Effective wrap-ups.

40. **Overcoming Obstacles—** Common hurdles to effective closings. How to prempt problems. Questioning and listening to a committment. How to follow up.

The Cdex Personal Computer Library   Training Needs

Programs	Entrepreneuring	Managing the Emerging Company	Managing the Larger Company	Strategic Planning	Company Structure	Managing By Objectives	Employee Productivity	Supervising Subordinates	Strategic Selling (Industrial)	Personal Managing Skills
1. Perspective On Managing	•	•	•			•				• •
2. Stages of Company Growth	•	•	•							
3. Setting Company Objectives	•	•	•	•	•	•	•			
4. Selecting Planning Units		•		•						
5. Managing the Planning Process		•		•						
6. Selecting a Planning Technique		•		•						
7. Basic Strategies for Building a Company	•	•		•	•					
8. Organizational Structures for Building a Company	•	•			•	•				
9. Productivity Fundamentals	•	•				•	•			•
10. Cultivating a Corporate Culture	•	•				•	•			
11. Perspective on Supervising								•	•	•
12. Setting Your Objectives	•					•		•		
13. Improving Productivity						•	•	•		•
14. Working with Individuals	•	•				•		•		•
15. Solving Day-To-Day Problems						•		•		•
16. Giving Day-To-Day Instructions						•		•		•
17. Training Your People						•	•	•		
18. Disciplining Your People						•	•	•		•
19. Delegating with Confidence	•					•		•		
20. Questioning & Listening	•					•	•	•		•

The Cdex Personal Computer Library   Training Needs

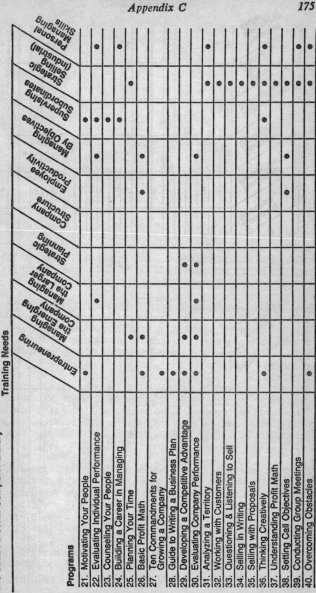

Programs	Entrepreneuring	Managing the Emerging Company	Managing the Larger Company	Strategic Planning	Company Structure	Employee Productivity	Managing By Objectives	Supervising Subordinates	Strategic Selling (Industrial)	Personal Managing Skills
21. Motivating Your People	●							●		
22. Evaluating Individual Performance			●				●	●		●
23. Counseling Your People								●		●
24. Building a Career in Managing		●						●		
25. Planning Your Time		●					●		●	
26. Basic Profit Math	●				●	●				
27. Ten Commandments for Growing a Company	●									
28. Guide to Writing a Business Plan	●									
29. Developing a Competitive Advantage	●			●						
30. Evaluating Company Performance	●			●						
31. Analyzing a Territory							●		●	●
32. Working with Customers									●	
33. Questioning & Listening to Sell									●	
34. Selling in Writing									●	
35. Selling with Proposals									●	
36. Thinking Creatively	●							●	●	●
37. Understanding Profit Math									●	
38. Setting Call Objectives						●			●	
39. Conducting Group Meetings							●		●	●
40. Overcoming Obstacles	●								●	●

EXHIBIT 2

Professional Authoring Software System

PASS is a dynamic authoring language for designing business training courseware. By combining multiple character sets, color graphics, video tape and video disk interface capabilities, branching, text editing and other features, PASS has the versatility to be used in varied business training applications.

With Bell & Howell's exclusive Professional Authoring Software System (PASS) you can develop customized, computer assisted instruction without computer programming experience. All prompts, in both authoring and lesson modes, are entirely in ENGLISH, so there is no need for either instructors or trainees to learn programming languages.

All courseware can be developed by following the step-by-step instructions in the PASS documentation, even sophisticated "branching" and graphics can be incorporated into lesson material without ever having to learn programming. All interaction can be accomplished simply by following the instructions as they appear on the display screen.

PASS includes a variety of testing methods and automatically keeps track of each learner's progress so you can monitor the effectiveness of each segment of courseware created with PASS.

Interactive Video

PASS helps you make your existing video materials interactive for added training impact. Because PASS enables your video tape and

Exhibit 2

video disk materials to interact with microcomputer equipment, your video based training programs become a more effective training medium. PASS informs, prompts and tests your trainees with video materials in sequences you determine. Learners may be "branched" through video lessons at their own pace with the microcomputer randomly accessing selected frames or sequences on your video disk or tape.

Video augmented managed interactive training offers you a means to increase the effectiveness of your current video training programs.

The Productivity Challenge

Productivity is the key challenge for the 1980's. With operating costs escalating because of inflation, businesses are becoming more and more concerned with increasing the productivity of their people.

Ultimately the day to day task of productivity improvement depends on the actions of individuals. Each employee must be committed to performance improvement in order for a company to see real productivity gains. To realize productivity potentials, employees must understand what they need to do as individuals to help the company reach its productivity goals. The company must be able to train its people to increase productivity while conducting this training efficiently and inexpensively.

Increasing productivity will be a primary concern of business and government during the 1980's. This task may be easier said than done, however it is possible to increase productivity while holding costs down . . . Bell & Howell has developed an exclusive system designed to help you train people to become more productive . . .

Training People to be More Productive

Bell & Howell's Managed Interactive Training System is a management tool that will help businesses achieve their productivity goals during the 80's.

As a supplier of training aids and information processing equipment, Bell & Howell has used its more than 40 years of training experience to design a powerful, microcomputer-based instructional system.

Exhibit 2

By combining a sophisticated and powerful authoring language called the Professional Authoring Software System (PASS) with the Bell & Howell microcomputer, Bell & Howell's unique Managed Interactive Training System is:

Interactive

PASS enables computer based training programs to be authored with complete interactive capability. The microcomputer "talks" to trainees in English, on an individual basis . . . branching rapid learners ahead, slowing the lesson for those needing review.

Computer Managed

Powerful computer routines inherent in the system enable the microcomputer to perform record keeping, grading and lesson management functions.

Cost Efficient

Bell & Howell's system allows the training process to be decentralized. People may be trained "on site" without expensive travel to a central training headquarters location. The microcomputer system and lesson material is inexpensive and completely portable.

Productivity Conscious

With the Bell & Howell microcomputer-based training system, training managers may devote more time to courseware design and management functions rather than training room instruction. Both the trainer and the training process become more productive.

Computer Assisted Instruction Offers Advantages Over Traditional Media

Computer Assisted Instruction (CAI) offers significant advantages over traditional training media. With CAI you have a learning system rather than a media device.

CAI allows for rapid changes in subject matter. Instructional modes and formats may be designed for any situation. As the information to be presented changes, computer-based materials are easily updatable. CAI lesson materials cost little to produce and may be distributed among multiple training sites inexpensively. Trainees at branch locations receive the same information as trainees in the home office. The material always has a uniform instructional quality. So from a cost efficiency standpoint CAI, and in particular, microcomputer based CAI, is a smart move for the trainer.

CAI increases the quality of instruction. Computers offer individualized instruction. Students work at their own pace. And because CAI is an interactive medium it forces learners to pay attention to lesson content. Trainees are tutored, prompted and then asked to respond to presented material. Material that was not learned can be immediately reviewed and reinforced until learning is complete.

Computers can be self-correcting. Programs can be designed to catch errors and correct mistakes instantly. They can diagnose weak areas by testing a specific skill and then assigning trainees to lessons. Trainees are given a consistent curriculum format so that each trainee learns all the material needed to perform the assigned task.

Instructors are relieved of much of their paperwork. The computer will handle enrollment, grading, progress analysis and many other record keeping tasks.

Why PASS?

PASS is a powerful, English-based authoring system that allows you to create CAI courseware without prior programming skills or knowledge. PASS prompts and questions the instructional designer. Its features make sophisticated programming skills available to anyone without the need to learn a programming language. PASS has an intelligent structure that allows anyone to author lessons with nearly unlimited flexibility.

Lessons are easily updated. A complete word processing system has been built into PASS. This allows you to quickly change words, or sentences, within lessons. Automatic grading and lesson analysis provides you with quality control and immediate validation.

Each student receives uniform instruction that has been individualized to meet their personal learning needs. PASS offers students self-paced, interactive, stimulating learning.

Let's compare PASS, an authoring system, to traditional computer programming. We feel PASS offers you both a more powerful, flexible learning system as well as being cost efficient. Here's why:

Exhibit 2

Authoring	Programming
• Prompts/Questions Author	• Blank Slate
• Has Pre-defined Authoring Format	• Total Configurability
• Contains Automatic Branching, Grading, Record Keeping	• Each Lesson Requires Branching, Grade Recording & Analysis Programs
• Intelligent Structure	• No Structure
• High Speed Lesson Execution	• Speed is a Problem
• Requires Little Production Time	• Requires Extensive Production Time

PASS lessons are easily and inexpensively reproduced. PASS is the ultimate training system for professional applications.

Exhibit 3

CONFIDENTIAL

RESUME

R.B. Brown
(Chairman & CEO)

Employment Background

1976–81 President, U.S. Management Development Corporation. Co-founded company and directed company growth to $16 million in sales. Negotiated successful sale of company to large, service-oriented conglomerate.

1970–76 V.P., Human Resources Development at General United Corporation (Fictitious name), a Fortune 500 company. Responsible for all phases of training, development and personnel.

1965–70 V.P., and General Manager of ABC Film Productions. Responsible for all programming and production. Profit responsibility included all phases of capital and expense budgeting at locations around the world. Company sales volume exceeded $40 million.

1958–65 Officer, U.S. Coast Guard.

Education

BSME, Purdue University, 1958
MBA, Golden Gate University, 1968

Personal

Married, two children. Mountain Climber.

EXHIBIT 3

CONFIDENTIAL

RESUME

W.L. Cliffton
(Candidate for President & COO Position)

Employment Background

1972–81 Vice President—Planning, National American Company, a leading ($2B sales) competitor in the office equipment industry. Responsible for budgeting and all phases of strategy development.

1967–72 President, Calcutronics Computer Corporation, a $60 million manufacturer of military systems.

1957–67 Senior Vice President, First National Bank of Los Angeles. Responsibilities included (at various times) data processing, marketing, and commercial lending.

Education

BA, University of Virginia, 1957
MBA, University of California, 1963
Southwestern Banking School, Southern Methodist University, 1966

Personal

Married. Jogger. Two books published.

Exhibit 3

CONFIDENTIAL

RESUME

Alice J. Fargo
(Candidate for Vice President—
Corporate Division)

Employment Background

1978–81 Senior Account Executive, LDI, Inc., a $100 million service company which provides economic forecasting to major companies. Progressed from position as sales representative to point where now responsible for over $4 million in annual revenues from a base of twenty-three clients.

1970–78 Sales Representative, IBM. Responsible for business products in Atlanta market.

1965–70 Customer Service Manager, A–M International in Chicago.

Education

BSEE, MIT, 1962

Personal

Peace Corps 1962–64. Knitter.

Epilogue to Appendix C

Venture Capitalists' Comments on the Cdex Corporation Business Plan

Ten professional venture capitalists reviewed the plan upon the request of the Cdex founders. Seven were from the west coast; two were from Chicago; one was New York City based. Five of the ten asked to see the detailed, confidential, financial plans that the Cdex management had developed with the help of a microcomputer and the Visicalc® software package. Following is a synopsis of the comments by the ten potential investors.

STRENGTHS

"Strong concept."

"Management appears to be balanced and appropriate for the business."

"Technology and timing look good."

"Understanding of production seems O.K."

"Market looks big . . . but hard to get to."

"Interesting idea. Pricing seems realistic."

"Programs are fantastic!"

"Training centers make a lot of sense."

"You're right. Micros are here to stay."

"Amazing gross margins."

"Excellent content in sample programs."

WEAKNESSES

"Distribution of finished products looks very messy. Very expensive."

"We don't like the marketing risk."

"Don't believe the sales projections (too high, too soon)."

"Too many unknowns in the training market."

"It's software. We don't invest in software. Only products."

"Price (for stock) is too high."

"You lack an experienced salesman at the top."

"I don't understand the business."

"You'll get drawn into custom programming—a service business."

"Weak linkage with Bell & Howell."

"Lacks analysis of competition—people like McGraw-Hill, Addison-Wesley, Apple Computer."

"No ROI information."

"Don't know of anyone who ever made money in the training business."

"Incomplete management team."

Of the ten potential investors, six said they were not interested ("no"). Most of these six indicated that Cdex just didn't fit their investment criteria. Cdex founders felt that there was a strong predisposition against "software" of any kind in this group.

Three of the remaining ten showed some interest. It varied from one firm's idea of hooking Cdex up with an existing company (in which the firm had an investment) that already had a program distribution network to another firm's request to be recontacted once several hundred thousand dollars in sales volume had been reached. This group seemed to smell an opportunity, but they were leery of the marketing/distribution challenges facing Cdex.

At the time this is being written, Cdex founders are still working with one of the ten potential investors. This particular investor has some personal background in publishing and human resource development. Together, the Cdex CEO and the venture capitalist are exploring several possible ways to "solve" the marketing/distribution issue at a reasonable cost. They currently share the view that Cdex can become a profitable $25,000,000 company in three to five years with an investment of under $1,000,000 and perhaps some selected additions to the product line and management team.

Editor's Note: At the time of printing, Cdex has raised over $1,000,000 in start-up capital based on a somewhat revised business plan and the addition of two co-founders to the management team.

Index